"In *Healing Racial Divides* Dr. Carter touches on the pulse of racialized issues challenging society and our sense of community. Carter uses thorough definitions and insightful examples of lived experiences to raise undeniable incongruities in perceptions that create border walls among humanity. Whether leader or laity, readers are convicted to ponder, *How did we move so far from God's loving-kindness?* Achieving solely that reflective outcome is worthwhile, yet Carter astutely moves us to hold up the mirror and ask,*What about me?"* —Valerie Miles-Tribble, Graduate Theological Union and American Baptist Seminary of the West

"Dr. Terrell Carter is an artist, pastor, educator, and former police officer. He combines these experiences with the insights of theology, the social sciences, law, and cultural analysis to address the key issue in America—the racial divide that inhibits our interactions and poisons public discourse. Carter's very personal engagement with the topic encourages us to find strength rather than division in our diversity. His approach is fresh, informative, and a source of healing." —Ircel Harrison, Central Baptist Theological Seminary and Pinnacle Associates

"As a pastor what I appreciate most is that Dr. Carter masterfully weaves his own painful personal experiences, scholarly research, biblical teaching, and the history of racial division into a book that is accessible and relevant to folks at any level of understanding in the conversation of racial inequality. His book is a great tool for any pastor or congregant seeking to begin or continue more deeply the important work of racial justice and healing." —Johnny Lewis, Shawnee Community Christian Church, Shawnee, Kansas

"While reading another substantive book by Dr. Carter, I'm resisting the urge to scribble quotes and shove them into the hands of anyone I can find. *Healing Racial Divides* is a unique contribution to healing racial brokenness due to Dr. Carter's rich and unique journey combined with keen academic insights. With precision, Dr. Carter strips away the illusion that racism is only historical in this country, yet his personal humility simultaneously disarms reader defensiveness. Ultimately, Dr. Carter calls the Church to live into its identity as a vessel of reconciliation in this divided world. I suspect many readers will mirror my experience, quoting this book most everywhere they can." —Mark E. Tidsworth, President, Pinnacle Leadership Associates

"Equipped with a pastor's heart, a scholar's mind, and a boundless sense of justice, Terrell Carter has provided a work that seeks first and foremost to change the very life of a community of faith. This text dares to address oft-ignored disparities and is approachable enough to offer practical ways that congregations can seek to fully embody their calling." — Tyler Tankersley, First Baptist Church, Cape Girardeau, Missouri

"*Healing Racial Divides* is a needed book. For some privileged communities, the racial divide is the third rail. Seek a closer look, get too close, and the community of polarized privilege will create more heat than light. Terrell Carter walks the racial divide with some ease as he seeks the light of understanding. This is a strong voice where the lines are drawn. Carter's closing chapter, 'Finding Common Ground,' shines brightly in the dark with its sense of wisdom and hope." —Keith Herron, St. Lucas United Church of Christ, St. Louis, author of *Living a Narrative Life: Essays on the Power of Stories*

"Dr. Carter uses a good blend of honest self-disclosure, personal and theological reflection, and historical recounting in this helpful book about racism and the road to recovery. He pulls us into our own culpability and points us unerringly in the direction of how to begin the journey to make things right. After reading Carter's words, I feel compelled to help both of us—along with all of our brothers and sisters—become the best versions of ourselves." —Robin R. Sandbothe, Englewood Baptist Church, and Director of Seminary Relations, Central Baptist Theological Seminary, Kansas City, Missouri

"Dr. Terrell Carter provides a must read for religious leaders who take seriously the call to bring awareness to the active, unequal racial systems of today. Combining both historical and biblical lenses, Carter encourages churches to lead the charge in which all are viewed as an equal child of God. This is a timely written book that should not only stand on a pastor's desk, but more importantly seep into a pastor's heart." —David McDaniel, Holmeswood Baptist Church, Kansas City, Missouri

Finding Strength in Our Diversity

healing racial divides

TERRELL CARTER

chalice
press

Saint Louis, Missouri

An imprint of Christian Board of Publication

ChalicePress.com

Print 9780827215122
EPUB 9780827215139
EPDF 9780827215146

Printed in the United States of America

This book is dedicated to the many people who supported me throughout the process of completing it.

To Brad Lyons and the staff at Chalice Press: Thank you for your patience as I completed the manuscript while juggling all the other things that life threw my way. I greatly appreciated your compassion and support.

To the congregations that have welcomed me and my family and allowed me to learn what it means to be a pastor, hopefully after God's own heart: Harmony Baptist Church, Broadway Baptist Church, Third Baptist Church, and Webster Groves Baptist Church. I have learned more from you than you have learned from me.

To the Carter clan for continual love and patience.

To Genevieve and Jerry for life more abundantly.

CONTENTS

ABOUT THE COVER

Author Terrell Carter discusses the artwork used on the cover:

The cover image, "Untitled," comes from a series of abstract images that I have been producing for several years that has culminated in a body of work titled "Good Negroes." The images, which are nondescript and faceless, can represent any person at any time. The only distinguishing features are the various colors used to form their bodies. The images represent the commonality that we all hold as human beings and, at the same time, the diversity that we all uniquely hold. They also represent my belief that we all originate from a common creator, and although we sometimes use our different physical aspects as ways to separate ourselves, in the end we all come from the One who sees us as the same.

My artistic style is influenced by artists from the Harlem Renaissance. Although many of those artists were classically trained in painting and drawing, they produced work that looked primitive and reflected their African heritage through angular colorful images. My hope, as was theirs, is to break long-held negative beliefs about African American culture and show that, although it may differ in many ways from white culture, it still holds multiple similarities.

Introduction

"Racism is particularly alive and well in America. It is America's original sin and it is institutionalized at all levels of society."[1]

Do we need another book about race? Another book about how divided our nation is? Can we not talk about something else, like *how to get along?*

Some would say that racism no longer exists because our nation finally elected its first African American president. Yet, in one of the more shocking developments during Obama's tenure as president, polls showed that 55 percent of adults believe that race relations within our nation, especially those between blacks and whites, worsened during his eight years in office.

Some might say that one of the biggest legacies left behind by the Obama administration is widespread racial division. When asked how serious a problem people thought racial discrimination against blacks was in the U.S., three out of four blacks said it was a problem, while two out of three whites said it was *not* a problem.[2] When asked if people thought that the country's criminal justice system treats whites and blacks equally, most white respondents said it did, but most black respondents said it did not. When asked about their feelings toward the Black Lives Matter movement and whether it was a good thing, 78 percent of African Americans thought the movement was a good thing that held a legitimate purpose, while 62 percent of whites said that it was *not* a good thing and did *not* have a legitimate purpose.

This division was quantified even more clearly by the general presidential election of 2016. For example, 88 percent

1

of African Americans voted for Clinton, while only 8 percent voted for Trump. One thing became very evident—issues of race played a key role in how people viewed the presidential candidates and what they hoped for from the next President. One thing the election results show is that, in general, blacks and whites see what is important for our communities, and the future of our country, *very differently*. We trust and distrust very different people.

This discussion relates to more than just black and white. But the historic relationship between blacks and whites serves as the primary example and the foundation for the discussion we must engage in. We must try to understand why we live in divided communities, cities, states, and nations. We must try to understand why police shootings of black men, whether armed or unarmed, continue to represent what black people believe is most wrong with the United States. We must try to understand why images of black people in criminal activity continue to be the ones primarily highlighted and pushed through various media platforms. This practice will be addressed in a subsequent chapter.

We must first discuss the different forms racism can take. Although it may not look like it did in the late nineteenth and early twentieth centuries, when people regularly and openly walked or rode around communities in white hoods while carrying torches, it still exists. We were reminded of this by the multiple white supremacists who proudly walked unhooded through the streets of Charlottesville, Virginia, in August 2017 wearing white supremacist regalia and carrying torches in protest of the removal of Confederate monuments.

We must discuss what we really think about black and brown people and the value they hold within our communities and organizations. And we must look at the way our nation perceives them as opposed to white people in similar circumstances.

It would seem there's a clear disparity in how most people feel about whites as opposed to minorities. For example:

- While at a local zoo, a first-grader from Wichita, Kansas, was mauled by a leopard after the boy scaled the four-foot railing that surrounded the leopard exhibit, crossed an eight-foot gap and approached the animal's cage. The child received lacerations to his head and neck after the leopard stuck its paw through the cage and grabbed the boy by the side of the head.[3]

• While at a Pittsburgh zoo, a two-year-old boy was mauled to death after he lunged from his mother's grasp and fell over a 10-foot wooden railing into the enclosed wild African dog exhibit. The child's family subsequently settled out of court with the zoo for an undisclosed sum.[4]

• While at Arkansas's Little Rock Zoo with his father and grandfather, a three-year-old boy slipped through the railings surrounding a jaguar exhibition and sustained multiple injuries after he fell 15 feet into the cat pit. The family's request to keep the child's name private was granted by the hospital, zoo, and multiple media outlets.[5]

• A two-year-old boy, while at a Cleveland zoo, suffered injuries to his legs after he experienced a 10-foot fall into a cheetah exhibit after his mother dangled him over the exhibit's railing.[6]

Outside of the fact that these incidents were heartbreakingly tragic, and they all occurred at zoos, the common factor was that neither the race of the child nor the race or criminal history of their parents ever became a point of emphasis by media outlets or the press after the circumstances were reported in the news. The children and families of the above stories were white.

In contrast, an African American child fell into a gorilla exhibit at the Cincinnati Zoo in 2016. The three-year-old boy, like some of the children in the prior stories, managed to get away from his mother and enter what was supposed to be a secure enclosure that would keep humans and animals separated. Unfortunately, this child made it past the initial security measures, which included a three-foot-tall fence and four feet of bushes, eventually falling 15 feet into a shallow moat in the gorilla enclosure. Harambe, a

17-year old gorilla, grabbed the boy and began to drag him. Zoo personnel, fearing for the boy's safety, shot and killed Harambe.[7]

Within hours of Harambe's death, most of the protests related to the incident were about the animal's death and not how the restricted area failed to keep the child out. The boy's mother was summarily vilified. People immediately questioned her fitness as a parent. Within days of the incident, the personal history and other information of the boy's father were being shared by media outlets on the internet. He was described as a thug and unfit to have children. One of the ironies of this was that the father was not at the zoo when his son tumbled into the enclosure. After finding out that the child and his parents were black, multiple outlets began to point to their race as a contributing factor for why the boy ended up in the predicament. In addition to their race, multiple pundits commented on the physical weight of the parents and the number of children in their family as additional contributing factors that likely played a part in why the child could slip away from his mother while at the zoo.

This is not the only time in recent history that white and black parents were portrayed differently in the media when their children were involved in similar unfortunate circumstances. "What passes as news for some (white) readers is simply lived experience for (black) others."[8]

For example, in St. Louis, a white infant died from heat exposure after her parents forgot that she was in the backseat of the family vehicle. The parents, who both worked for a prominent medical facility, drove to work that fateful day with their daughter in the back seat. Both parents exited the car thinking that the other had unbuckled their daughter and removed her from her car seat.[9]

Tragically, they were both wrong. In the end, the parents were not charged with a crime related to her death. Instead, the public was encouraged to show that family sympathy. Both parents were white and well-to-do. Less than a week later, a single black mother was arrested after she left her adolescent children in an air-conditioned car while she ran into a store to grab a few items. This woman was summarily vilified in the media. Emphasis was placed on the fact that she had "too many" children and should have made other arrangements to keep her children safe. These incidents must be discussed. Why do black people and other minorities not receive the benefit of the doubt in incidents like this, while white people do? I agree with Gayraud Wilmore's suggestion that racism may not be intentional. He says, "It exists with or without sophisticated theories and systematic rationalizations. It can be conscious or unconscious, continuous or sporadic."[10] Yet I can't help but think it's also intentional and systematic.

Many times, your side in this argument is based on your race. How do we who seek justice and equality for all people, regardless of race, help to change this?

This is a reason I am writing another book on race: because, the issue in our country has not gotten much better. Things have gotten better in some areas for blacks, but more needs to occur for us to know we are fully equal. Historian David Katzman said there is "a tragic sameness in the lives of black people today and in the past. In spite of all the changes in American society—the weakened proscription, the increased influence, the improved education—so much of the quality of black life remains dependent upon the rest of society and is disturbingly inferior to that of white people."[11] Yes, we may have elected our first black President, but he was still treated like a second-class citizen by some, had his very citizenship ridiculously denied by some, and his ethnicity was regularly a point of contention, especially within white evangelical Christian culture.

I write this book to participate in bridging the divide in our nation. Although we have been dealing with this subject for centuries, no clear solution has been identified. That should not preclude us from continuing the conversation. We must work through old and current ideas for us to find common ground.

There are other reasons:

Our churches are still divided.

I don't set out to see life through race-colored glasses, but sometimes it's hard not to. At a recent meeting for our denomination, a white woman asked, "Why don't more black men attend our churches?" Although the denomination loves people of all races and has made concerted efforts to increase the diversity of people groups attending its meetings, minority representation at the event I was attending was scant. This has been true of all the events that I have attended for the group in the past.

"We can't get black men, or many black people in general, to come to our church or participate in our events," she explained. "Can you help me understand why?" There are multiple reasons—there may be a black church already in the community, but there's another big reason too. The answer I offered was based on my experience of being the lone minority, or one of the few attending a predominantly white service or event.

I told her I know that when I enter any space comprised primarily of white people, I am viewed as a suspect. As soon as I walk through the door, people wonder who I am and what I'm doing there. The uneasy looks I receive, the half-hearted handshakes, the roundabout questions to gauge my intentions, this only ends when I introduce myself as Dr. Carter, a seminary professor and pastor.

Second, typically when white churches and leaders communicate, it is *at* me, and not *with* me. The white pastor or leader is the expert and I am the learner, regardless of the subject. This is also reflected in how some whites view black church experiences. They describe black church life in emotional terms, while white church life is described in intellectual terms. Black church is where people sing, shout, and "feel" the Lord, while white church is where a person's intellect is challenged, as if any of these things are exclusive of one another.

Third, my experience has been that black people are asked to "come to whites," while whites do not necessarily come to us. When a white congregation wants to build a relationship with a black person or church, we are asked to meet them at their facilities or their place of choice. "White pastors always invite me to meet them at a Starbucks," a pastor friend told me. "I understand it's where they feel comfortable, but I don't drink coffee and I don't live or serve in the suburbs." His experiences are not unique. These types of things happen when any church or group attempts to interact with or build relationships with millennials, gays and lesbians, or any other group different from them.

We all need to learn about people different from us.

The need to learn how to interact with many people has always been an important way to live the gospel. Jesus built his reputation upon the fact that he was willing to not only interact with, but also embrace, people who were considered outcast and other. In the gospels, Jesus had to regularly contend with what people thought of him and those he regularly surrounded himself with. Whether fishermen, tax collectors, or the sick, these were the "wrong" kind of people. In Luke 7:36–50, he answers the religious elites' question head-on during a meal at the home of Simon the Pharisee.

One of the customs of the day was when an influential leader or teacher came to your home, you left the door open and allowed people to come in and hear what that person was saying. People did come to hear Jesus, including a woman who is described only as "a sinner." In Jesus' day, you could be classified as a sinner even if there was evidence to the contrary. If your life circumstances were less than perfect or something especially bad happened to you, people would attribute your misfortune to a hidden sin in your life.

After entering Simon's residence, the woman uses her hair, her tears, and a bottle of expensive perfume to clean Jesus' dusty feet. It was a humiliating and scandalous act that any righteous person could not overlook. Simon, the most righteous person present, is appalled at the woman and at Jesus for letting her touch him. Jesus asks, "Who do you think appreciates it more when their sin is forgiven, someone who has been forgiven for a little or a lot?" Simon says, "The one forgiven for a lot."

Jesus agrees and reminds him that he forgot to engage in the simplest graces typically exhibited by a dinner host: offering to wash a guest's feet. "This woman not only cleaned my feet," he says. "She hasn't stopped kissing them since she arrived. The true embarrassment is not in her actions but in the attitude you have toward her and toward me." The passage ends with Jesus pronouncing the unilateral forgiveness of her sins, whatever they may be.

I must acknowledge I see some of Simon in me. I imagine you do too. We are sometimes quick to pass judgment on others whose life circumstances are not like ours. Episcopal priest David Sellery says, "For all of us, there is a certain, secret satisfaction knowing that there is a bigger sinner somewhere…down the street, around the corner or at the next desk."[12] I forget that God even calls them beloved.

"The sinner" is usually the person we think is different. That person is not as "righteous" as we are or doesn't exhibit the same qualities or accomplishments. But, no matter how worthy we consider ourselves, God sees all of us as we are, as people forgiven for *a lot*, and with a lot to be thankful for. One of the hardest things for righteous people to do is invite those different from us into our world. However, this is what Jesus did, regardless of what it did to his reputation.

Like Simon, I can be judgmental of people I consider sinful or "other." But, I also recognize myself in the sinful woman. I have been an outsider among judgmental people. I know how it feels to walk into a room and feel judged because of my skin color, or the neighborhood where I grew up, or my family circumstances. I was raised by my paternal grandparents. They had my father when they were 16 years old. Neither of them went to high school. In turn, my parents became pregnant with me and my twin brother when they were 17 years old, and neither of them graduated high school.

We grew up in a predominantly African American neighborhood called the Ville in North St. Louis City. "What good can come from Nazareth?" What good can come from the Ville? The Ville is a neighborhood some people would consider unacceptable, one of those neighborhoods in which my white friends might ask, "Is it safe?" When a white person hears about my life, they say, "You turned out well despite your beginning." It may be unintentional, but it reveals the same kind of attitude Simon held toward the sinful woman.

Theological educator John Martens says, "It is we who define ourselves as 'worthy' by creating distinctions between those whom we consider 'real' sinners and those whom we judge basically 'righteous,' which generally includes me and those like me."[13] The sinner, the other, the person unworthy to be in my presence is the one different from me, whether they mean to be different or not. I am thankful my personal value is not eternally determined by others' perceptions of me, the family I was born into, where I grew up, or the challenges I have experienced. My value is based on something greater: God's love for me through Jesus' sacrificial life, death, and resurrection. My value comes from God's affirmation of me as a child of the King. And, the same applies to you.

Our struggles are spiritual and racial.

Have you ever played tug-of-war? Romans 7 speaks of a spiritual tug-of-war in our relationship to God, and others. One of Paul's goals was to help readers understand how these relationships form Christ's body on the earth. He argues that, although we've become part of Christ's body, we still face the ghosts of law and sin that previously controlled our lives. God's commands and any disobedience of them would lead to consequences we'd all have to face one day. However, the good news is that Jesus changed the trajectory of history and freed us from condemnation to be restored to full relationship with God, despite our being unable to fulfill the law or live sinless. Through Christ, we are no longer condemned by the law.

Yet Paul said there would still be this spiritual tug-of-war, going back and forth between what God wants versus what we want. He said we know what God wants, and even when we want to do it, the flesh fights against it. We want to please God, but our hearts and minds somehow work against us. That is one of the things I most appreciate about Paul's writings. He doesn't try to sugarcoat the challenges we will face in life. He doesn't say once you have accepted Christ, life becomes perfect. He says the opposite. *Because* we have accepted Christ as Savior, life will in some ways get harder because we're attempting to live up to a higher standard of love. Proper faith or proper relationship with God recognizes you will sometimes fail; however, even in those times, you can still get life right when you know you can't do it by yourself. You must seek God's face for assistance.

This is not a cop out or a less-godly standard. It's acknowledging people are still human and, as Paul said, the fact that the things we know we should do, we don't always do. Thank God our story doesn't end there. I find joy in Paul's final words: our hope is not in ourselves, but in Jesus, who will ultimately cause us to be victorious in this spiritual tug-of-war. I write this book to have yet another conversation about race, in the hope that we can be honest about ourselves and our views of others, and realize that the sin of racism is one sign we are failing to live up to the standard Jesus set. I hope to remind people we all play a part in either keeping the sin of racism going, or ending it.

"The central social and hence theological issue of our time is the crisis of racial and cultural alienation and no appeal exclusively to the standards of our faith and witness will meet that social obligation."[14] If we all would be honest about the part we play, we could do a better job of working together to destroy this alienation and reflect God's love for everyone. I hope that after engaging with the ideas found in this book, readers will recommit to focusing energy toward understanding others and finding common ground.

We must name our own sin(s) before we can point a finger at others.

The story is told of a Caucasian woman who, after boarding a flight from South Africa to England, realized her seatmate was a dark-skinned African man. She was not pleased with this arrangement and expressed her displeasure to a flight attendant. The woman said that she was willing to pay for a first-class seat so she did not have to sit next to this African man. The flight attendant walked to the first-class cabin and had a brief discussion with the crew. A few minutes later the attendant returned. She leaned over and said to the African man, "I am sorry to have to do this. I need to make a seating change. If you follow me, we have a place for you in first class."

Most of us would likely be embarrassed if this incident occurred on a flight we were on. We would feel sorry for the man and also likely a sense of vindication as the man reclined in first class while the woman remained in coach. We'd feel anger, maybe even sorrow, about the outdated thinking and might even voice our displeasure. I imagine most would feel righteous indignation toward the woman.

Yet are we willing to consider that sometimes we exhibit the same mindset as that woman? We may not voice it, but we feel superior to those who do not "fit our standards," are poor, or are simply different from us.

Jonah experienced righteous indignation after God spared Nineveh. He believed he was justified. Such an indignant attitude is a problem in the twenty-first century as well. "If you are not on *our* side or do not believe exactly as I believe, you are my enemy," some would say, adding: "and I hope things go wrong in your life." Fortunately, this is not God's mode of operation with us. God is patient, even with those not considered members of the "redeemed." That's just the way God is. God's love does not end with us. It may be more visible through our relationship with God, but it does not begin or end with us.

As with Jonah, God implores us to reach out to others and show love to them as well. God sends us into people's lives to reinforce that love and to be examples for them to see and follow. This is what Jonah couldn't bring himself to accept. I pray we will be more faithful to this shared opportunity. I hope to be more faithful than Jonah.

Our personal monuments are sometimes more important to us than God's.

Have you ever been mistaken for someone else? This happens to me on a regular basis—for a few reasons. The first is because I have an identical twin brother. We were born 12 minutes apart and we look, sound, and act alike. For a few years, we worked three blocks from each other in downtown St. Louis and, on a weekly basis, someone would inevitably mistake him for me and vice versa. The second reason is because I share the same name with a famous singer and actor. When people Google his name, they sometimes reach out in hopes of locating the "real" Terrell Carter.

More recently, I have been mistaken for the "wrong kind of Christian." When people ask what I do professionally, I tell them I am a professor and a pastor. Inevitably, some experience an immediate change of attitude and I want to qualify my statement. "But I'm not *that* kind of Christian."

During the month of August, a pastor friend responded to a call for clergy to travel to Charlottesville, Virginia, in response to white supremacists gathering to defend a Robert E. Lee statue in the city specifically, and all Confederate monuments in general. My friend said that on the first day he was glad to see a group of police officers coming toward him in full riot gear with weapons. He believed they'd provide crowd control. Unfortunately, as this group continued to approach, he realized that though they had matching uniforms and even weapons, they weren't police, but the white supremacist militia there to protect what they considered sacred monuments.

This idea of mistaken identity is important to me because, truthfully, Christians have become known less for protecting the practices of Jesus and more for protecting political monuments. But, as I begin to cast stones, I must pause and ask myself, *Am I any better than them?* What monuments in my life do I protect? I do the same things they do, just for other monuments. If we all would be honest and think deeply, we could each identify "monuments" in our lives, as well. We all hold onto some things in ways that, if challenged, would likely not be identified as behavior befitting "children of the king."

I hope to challenge you to address the monuments you protect—those built around antiquated and unhelpful concepts of race that cause harm to you and others. I hope to encourage you to be willing to turn them over to God for removal so they no longer hinder you from reflecting the love and grace of our Creator.

Heaven will be more diverse than we can imagine.

What comes to mind when you think of the kingdom of heaven? Based on the visions of Old Testament prophets and descriptions found in the book of Revelation, most of us think of a physical place. Even Jesus said there are many dwelling places in his "Father's house." But what if there is more to heaven than just a physical place that awaits us on the other side? I think that's partly what Jesus is talking about in the parables in Matthew 13.

When Jesus used the phrase "kingdom of heaven," he was not talking about heaven only as our final resting place, but ultimately was describing what it meant for God to be present with people, especially in the here and now. The kingdom of heaven is like a small mustard seed, a small amount of leaven (yeast), an unnamed treasure in a field, and an expensive pearl.

Jesus' listeners would not have viewed mustard seeds or leaven as good things. They both were nuisances that corrupted their surroundings. Heaven was a weed people would be disappointed in and want to get rid of. Heaven was more likely to be thrown away than used.

Jesus suggests heaven is like a man who buys a field because he found a great treasure in it, but doesn't tell the original owner. That sounds like a shady business practice to me. And, it's like a jeweler who, hunting for a bargain, comes across a pearl worth more than any he already has, and sells everything, essentially bankrupting himself, to buy it.

In these parables, Jesus uses questionable images to show that the kingdom of heaven would start small and grow into something people could never imagine. The stories of questionable business practices show that the people that make up the kingdom hold tremendous value in God's eyes—so much so that heaven would send its greatest gift as a sacrifice to restore right relationship with God.

If this is what heaven is about, God's body represented in a small band of believers, and God's willingness to pay for it through the sacrifice of the Son, can that change our view of heaven? Heaven may not be only a place off in the distance, but also something available to all *right now* through the sacrificial work of Christ. Maybe this kingdom can become recognizable in the world through how its members embody God's love. People may see heaven as the people and relationships that represent God. That's the kind of kingdom I want to be part of.

Unity in how we live with each other is a sign of spiritual maturity.

President Obama will not be the only person with a legacy of racial division. There has been an even clearer divide along racial lines after the election of Donald Trump. Many have family members, friends, and coworkers they no longer speak to because they voted differently. Yet many people who no longer speak to each other on Facebook or in public continue to attend church together and worship God in the same place.

Paul dealt with this problem in 1 Corinthians 1:10–18, writing to believers who disagreed with each other. Paul wanted to help them navigate the messiness that occurs when people don't see eye to eye, but live and worship together. Word had gotten back to him that arguments were happening around "who baptized whom"—Cephas, Apollos, Paul? People were missing the point. It didn't matter *who* because all three were baptizing in the name of the same Lord. Their arguments implied they didn't have a proper foundation of faith in the first place.

Rev. Paul Bellan-Boyer says the church at Corinth had the wrong spirit. "The problem is not that they have a different household in faith, but that they are quarreling. This points out that they lack the kind of unity which Paul presumes is a fruit of belonging to Christ. Clothing yourself with Christ does not erase our differences, but it does cover them, sets them aside, puts them in a new context."[15] So, the problem was not that they had differences. The problem was that they had allowed their differences to become the priority.

Members of the body of Christ can be on opposing sides of so many different things. Rev. Mary Hinkle Shore says, "Unity of mind and purpose comes, not because a particular leader is able to create consensus, or because all possess knowledge or some other spiritual gift. Rather, the unity that Paul urges on the Corinthians is born from a baptism that connects all participants to Christ's death and resurrection."[16]

Spiritual maturity is seen in our ability not to let disagreements cause us to separate, but instead help us draw closer and be reminded of our common foundation. Dr. Dwight Peterson says, "Unity, of course, does not mean uniformity. But it does mean that the church ought not allow itself to be divided by things like human leaders, but instead ought to keep the Gospel and the power of the cross of Christ firmly in view."[17] My ultimate hope and prayer is that this book will bring people together and serve as encouragement for those in community with others different from themselves.

I also hope to challenge the white church and contemporary evangelical culture around the perceptions often held, sometimes unintentionally, that black and brown people "need to be saved from themselves," to be taught the "correct" way to be Christian, or that black and brown people are experts on poverty, social struggle, and the like, but not of scripture.

I write as a black man told by white teachers there were certain things I could and could not do because I was *black*. And, these messages did not end when I left elementary school. My twin brother, after earning four master's degrees, was hired to lead a department for a company in the Midwest, but was told by a white subordinate he was simply the latest "affirmative action hire." Having won more industry awards in the field than the entire department didn't matter. This wasn't 1990 or 2000. It happened after 2010.

Such experiences may not be the standard experiences of all black people. But, they are for more black people than not. Race does not play a factor in every experience. Class and sex play roles as well. But, we need to try to see racism for what it is.

Racism is not the explanation for everything black people face, but we can't overlook the past racist actions that have shaped our communities, states, and nation. "One of the enduring realities of life is that majorities discriminate against minorities, especially where race or ethnicity is concerned. Each of us likes to believe that God especially loves our group and its ways. We feel suspicious and threatened by other kinds of people. The unfortunate result is discrimination."[18]

I also write this book from the privileged vantage point of serving as the first African American pastor of two historically white churches, one of which formed specifically to serve white Christians who wanted to worship separately. Although both churches learned to love people of all races and ethnicities, diversity happened as a conscious decision to invite people unlike those already in the congregation.

Finally, I hope to offer those seeking informed pastoral engagement an understanding of how the past may contribute to the discussion of race and our relationships. Yet, rather than point at villains and lay blame, I hope that we seek to remember both sides are filled with human beings who inhabit a fallen world and are themselves products of fallen, sinful people. In this messy game of spiritual tug-of-war, we can all too easily forget we are not the only ones on the side of righteousness, and those who disagree with us are not far from God's side.

I hope you will be emboldened to continue in this critical journey with me.

Terrell Carter, D.Min.
April 2018

1

Roots of Our Racial Division

"I still think today as yesterday that the color line is a great problem of this century. But today I see more clearly than yesterday that back of the problem of race and color, lies a greater problem which both obscures and implements it: and that is the fact that so many civilized persons are willing to live in comfort even if the price of this is poverty, ignorance, and disease of the majority of their fellowmen."

—W.E.B. Du Bois[1]

When you were in high school, what table did you sit at when you ate lunch in the cafeteria? If you went to a high school such as mine, Gatesville Senior High, home of the Fighting Hornets, you had a certain table that you were expected to sit at. And, only certain people would sit at that table with you. The table where you sat symbolized your social status. It represented where you stood in the food chain of life at Gatesville High School, and everyone had a place. More specifically, everyone had a *table*. Athletes had a table. Preppy kids had a table. Cheerleaders had a table. The smokers stood outside by a dumpster behind the cafeteria. It would take an act of God, or by one of the cool kids, to help you move. If you tried to sit at a different table on your own, there could be severe social consequences.

So, what table did you sit at? Or, a better question may be: At what table do you sit *now*? You still can have certain expectations placed upon you by the group you associate with. Much of the underlying tension our nation experiences stems from this separating along social and economic lines.

Who are you not expected to sit with? What type of person makes you cringe when you see them coming your way? Is it someone with a lot of tattoos? Could it be a black or brown woman with a group of children? A police officer?

If you grew up in Gatesville, Texas, it was anyone who came from McGregor, Texas. McGregor is located 20 miles east of Gatesville, and the only good thing about the town of McGregor (to *my* mind, back then) was the fact that the highway that led to Waco, Texas, went through McGregor. When I lived in Gatesville, the two towns despised each other. The relationship between Gatesville and McGregor was like the Hatfields and McCoys. We did not like them and they did not like us.

Part of the reason for this was because Gatesville could not beat McGregor in anything. They whupped us in every sport. From football to basketball to baseball to track. They were always bigger than us, stronger than us, and faster than us. We were smarter and more creative than them, but nobody wanted to brag about the fact that we beat them in our regional headline writing competition. If one of our friends moved from Gatesville to McGregor, they became *persona non grata* to us.

This act of treating people differently based on where their family lives, or their town of origin, is not a new phenomenon. No matter how old you are, you've probably known a story like this since you were a child. We find multiple examples in the Book of Acts in the New Testament. Specifically, in Acts 11, the disciple Peter almost got into serious trouble with the religious people of his day for simply eating with the "wrong" people.

Imagine: instead of dirt roads from the Bible, a two-lane highway runs through town. And, instead of donkeys, there are pick-up trucks, and the local Walmart and the Texas

Department of Corrections at the edge of town are the two places everyone works.

Now imagine Peter is the president of the campus Fellowship of Christian Athletes, and he's just returned from a trip where he met with people from McGregor High School, the sworn enemies of any proud Fighting Hornet. When Peter sits down in the cafeteria for lunch, he is confronted by members of the debate team. The boys are a force to be reckoned with, and they're keen to give Peter a piece of their minds for breaking the rules and spending time with their enemies. The head of the debate team steps forward and tells Peter they've heard he's had lunch with a McGregor Bulldog.

Who Would Jesus Hate?

There was no love between Jews and Gentiles during the time of the early church. They did not like each other, and they did not trust each other. It was not that Jews and Gentiles never mixed. Truthfully, most Jews did not have a choice but to live in a world full of people who were not of their heritage. Jews and Gentiles lived life together, whether they liked it or not. Now, one of the challenges for Jews was adhering to the idea of being "clean." For them, the idea of being clean stemmed from multiple requirements given by God in Leviticus to address certain actions that would make a person unclean and unacceptable before God. In Leviticus 11—26, God gave 613 rules the children of Israel were to follow to stay clean.

There were many things that could make you unclean, and thus unacceptable before God—things such as getting too close to a dead body, bearing a child, or eating certain foods. It was understood that no one could keep the purity laws perfectly, so there were provisions for becoming clean again. For Peter, the bigger problem was that he'd willingly gone to a Gentile's home and eaten with him.

The purity laws lent themselves to a spiritual hierarchy between those who considered themselves close to God, and the "unclean," who were shunned as impure sinners. Instead of expressing the holiness of God, the practice of being pure became a means of excluding people. Following these rules became a way to justify keeping certain people out and believing them far from God. By voluntarily doing what he did, Peter was bucking that system.

The traditions that have shaped our nation have been used to keep groups of people separated from each other. Specifically, they have been used to keep one group of people in power over and above multiple others. Beliefs, laws, policies, and practices have been created by whites and used to keep black people enslaved and subjugated for years. The effects of those laws are still being felt in the twenty-first century.

Before we look at this system of racial oppression, we need to define some words.

Race—A group of people possessing certain physical characteristics in common determined by heredity.

Races, historically, are the descriptions for people of color developed as white racial identity was itself being established. First came the transatlantic slave trade, and then came the scientific language of race, which helped organize Western societies around that very lucrative practice. Race is a myth biologically, but it is a political reality. Racism is the effort to create and sustain systems and structures for whites. Race is a financially incentivized anthropology designed to legitimize the buying, selling, and owning of African bodies.[2]

Racism–Racism is more than just a personal attitude. It is the institutionalized form of that attitude. It is "the dogma that one ethnic group is condemned by nature to congenital inferiority and another group to congenital superiority."[3]

Racism as an ideology is founded on two myths, which have permeated human social relations for centuries. By *myth* here I mean, "a notion based more on tradition or convenience than on fact." One myth is that there is something called European "white" civilization which over time evolved to become the highest form of human development and cultural refinement and by which standard all other races and cultures must be judged, measured or assessed. The myth asserts that this European civilization is founded on Judeo-Christian values and has been destined to lead the world towards the achievement of the highest levels of human development.[4]

Racism is racial prejudice plus power. Racism is the intentional or unintentional use of power to isolate, separate, and exploit others. This use of power is based on a belief in superior racial origin, identity or supposed racial characteristics. Racism confers certain privileges on and defends the dominant group, which in turn sustains and perpetuates racism. Both consciously and unconsciously, racism is enforced and maintained by the legal, cultural, religious, educational, economic, political, and military institutions of societies.[5]

Institutional racism is one of the ways organizations and structures serve to preserve injustice. Intended or not, the mechanisms and function of these entities create a pattern of racial injustice.

Racism is one of several sub-systems of domination in the modern world. It interacts with other sub-systems to produce broad patterns of oppression and exploitation that plague the world. Among these sub-systems are class and sexual oppression. Women who are also victimized by racism face a compound burden. They not only have to deal with oppression due to their racial origin or identity, but they are also confronted with economic and political exploitation and oppression based on their sex and/or class.[6]

Prejudice – "Prejudice is a personal attitude toward other people based on a categorical judgement about their physical characteristics, such as race or ethnic origin."[7]

With those definitions in place, we can begin to look at how certain scientific and social theories, such as

Darwinism, influenced several strategic events related to race conversations and thinking—including the Dred Scott decision, the 13th Amendment loophole, and Jim Crow laws—to justify slavery.

The Influence of Darwinism

Historically, the theory of evolution has been used to justify viewing people of some races as inferior to others. The theory of evolution was heavily influenced by the book *Vestiges of the Natural History of Creation,* written by Robert Chambers. Scottish-born Chambers wore many hats in his lifetime, including that of publisher, geologist, and journal editor. He was highly influential within mid-nineteenth–century scientific and political circles. Chambers believed: "Various races of mankind, are simply...stages in the development of the highest or Caucasian type...and that the Blacks were the least developed, and the Caucasians were the highest, most evolved race."[8] In the end, *Vestiges* proposed a theory of social and biological evolution that concluded: "The Negro was 'at the foot of' the Mongol, the Yellow race between, and Caucasians at the top."

Charles Darwin, a geologist and biologist, built on this theory within his book *On the Origin of Species by Means of Natural Selection, or the Preservation of Favoured Races in the Struggle for Life. On the Origin of Species* posited that, through the process of natural selection, some groups and/or populations learn necessary skills to evolve and/or change over time, while other groups/populations do not. He applied this theory specifically to people.

One of the interesting things about Darwin's personal life is that he was opposed to all forms of slavery. However, this personal belief did not stop him from concluding that one of the strongest evidences for evolution was the existence of living 'primitive races,' which he believed were evolutionarily between the 'civilized races of man' and the gorilla. After making contact with the Indian population of Tierra del Fuego, Darwin wrote, "I could not have believed how wide was the difference between savage and civilized man; it is greater than between a wild and domesticated animal... Viewing such a man, one can hardly make oneself believe that they are fellow creatures and inhabitants of the same world."[9]

In Darwin's view, the civilized races (whites) would eventually replace the savage races (all other races) throughout the world. Darwin saw this natural selection coming to fruition in multiple ways. He saw it in action through the killing of the indigenous peoples of Australia by British forces. He saw the black race as one of the "savage races" and categorized them as being closer in kin to gorillas than to other humans. He also advocated against social programs that benefited the poor and weak because he believed such programs permitted the least desirable people in the gene pool to survive when they should be allowed to die off.

Darwin wrote:

> At some future period, not very distant as measured by centuries, the civilized races of man (White) will almost certainly exterminate, and replace, the savage races (Black) throughout the world. At the same time, the anthropomorphous apes...will no doubt be exterminated. The break between man and his nearest allies will then be wider, for it will intervene between man in a more civilized state, as we may hope, even than the Caucasian, and some ape as low as a baboon, instead of as now between the Negro or Australian and the gorilla... It has often been said...that man can resist with impunity the greatest diversities of climate and other changes; but this is true only of the civilized races.[10]

By the late 1800s, Darwin's theory of evolution had spawned Social Darwinism. Quickly after its inception, Social Darwinism began to take hold of society's collective thinking. Social Darwinists took the ideas found in Darwinism and evolved them to argue forcefully that certain inferior races were less evolved, or less human because those who were "less evolved" were more akin to apes than to normal humans. With Darwinism as their model, social scientists Herbert Spencer and William Graham Sumner argued that a society's existence was a life-and-death struggle in which the best individuals would eventually overcome inferior individuals. Sumner argued that wealthy Americans, almost all of whom were white, were the beneficiaries of natural selection and, as the superior race, were necessary to the advancement of civilization. Africans and their descendants were viewed as a degenerate race.

Additionally, there was the belief that one of the drawbacks of evolution was the idea that the existence of racially inferior people groups was unavoidable. This idea appeared in many of the biology textbooks that were being used at the time. *A Civic Biology*, a trusted American high school textbook, included a section on evolution under the subtitle "The Races of Man." The section identified the five races or varieties of people. Each race was very different from the others in instinct, social customs, and structure. It should not be hard to guess which group was at the top and which was at the bottom. "There are the Ethiopian or Negro type, originating in Africa; the Malay or brown race, from the islands of the Pacific; the American Indian; the Mongolian or yellow race, including the natives of China, Japan and the Eskimos; and finally, the highest type of all, the Caucasians, represented by the civilized white inhabitants of Europe and America."[11]

A Civic Biology was not unique. Most textbooks described blacks as physically and mentally inferior to most other races. The book *The Negro: A Menace to American Civilization* stated:

> By the nearly unanimous consent of anthropologists this type occupies...the lowest position in the evolutionary scale... [T]he cranial sutures...close much earlier in the Negro than in other races. To this premature ossification of the skull, preventing all further development of the brain, many pathologists have attributed the inherent mental inferiority of the blacks, an inferiority which is even more marked than

their physical differences… [T]he development of the Negro and White proceeds on different lines… [I]n the former the growth of the brain is…arrested by the premature closing of the cranial sutures… The mental [differences] are at least as marked as the physical differences… No full-blooded Negro has ever been distinguished as a man of science, a poet, or an artist.[12]

Thomas Huxley, an early proponent and defender of evolution and believer in the physical and social superiority of the White race, wrote:

No rational man, cognizant of the facts, believes that the average Negro is the equal, still less the superior, of the white man. And, if this be true, it is simply incredible [to assume] that, when all his disabilities are removed…he will be able to compete successfully with his bigger-brained and smaller-jawed rival, in a contest which is to be carried out by thoughts and not by bites.[13]

The Social Sciences

Whether intentionally or unintentionally, the social sciences have also contributed to extensively lengthening the divide between blacks and whites. One example is the study published as *The Bell Curve: Intelligence and Class Structure in American Life*. The study argued that human intelligence is substantially affected by multiple inherited and environmental factors and is the best predictor of how a person will behave in life, especially as it relates to the personal dynamics of income, job performance, birth out of wedlock, and involvement in crime. The authors also argue that people with high intelligence are successively finding themselves separated from those of average and below-average intelligence.

The authors, Richard Herrnstein and Charles Murray, claimed that inherited intelligence was the primary determining factor for how a person turned out in life, and not their environment or social class. They wrote that "success or failure in the American economy, and all that goes with it, are increasingly a matter of the genes that people inherit."[14] They also stated: "The poor are poor not because they are unlucky to be born poor, but because they were not lucky enough to have inherited good genes."[15] The authors also stated that IQ tests and scores were the most reliable way of learning and measuring a person's cognitive ability. They also claimed that a person's cognitive ability likely could not be improved.

Through their research, they argued that people within the United States were naturally self-selecting and separating among themselves based on cognitive abilities. Those with high IQs were forming a group of "cognitive elites," and those who were not as mentally astute were finding themselves as members of the inferior class. Those with high IQs were destined to experience wealth and upward mobility, while those with low IQs were destined to experience lives marred by poverty, unemployment, crime, and dependence on government assistance.

The authors used their accumulated data to suggest that certain social programs, those that primarily benefited African Americans, needed to be ended or have their funding severely slashed because those programs only helped to subsidize the continuation of a population with lower intelligence and lower life expectations. The groups they were primarily referring to were African Americans and Latino/as. The authors wrote, "The ranks of the cognitively inferior are disproportionately filled with blacks, Latinos, and today's immigrants. And that's a serious disadvantage because low IQ—not education or opportunity—is the key factor underlying problems ranging from poverty and criminal behavior to out of wedlock births and being a bad parent."[16]

Obviously, not everyone agreed with their findings. In the article "Flattening the Bell Curve," journalist Joe Sims wrote:

> The racist proposals put forward in The Bell Curve are more than just talk. They are increasingly becoming governmental policy. The Republican Contract on America is *The Bell Curve* in legislative form. One

of the main planks in the contract is the so-called Personal Responsibility Act whose intent is clear: eliminate welfare to lower birthrates among African American and Latino women.

...The Bell Curve is a direct challenge to the concept of human equality. Inequality is said to be immutable and determined by heredity... The ideological generals of the right wing admit as much. Here are two examples. Pat Buchanan said, "I think a lot of the data [in *The Bell Curve*] is indisputable... It does shoot a hole straight through the heart of egalitarian socialism which tried to create equality of result by coercive government programs.[17]

Mr. Sims' argument against *The Bell Curve* study is that it implies governmental funding through social services is not helpful because certain groups of people, unfortunately, are not as equal as others. I believe he's right and that the study smacks of Darwinistic thinking.

Medical Experimentation

There is a long history of medical experimentation on black bodies in America. We know about some of these experiments because they were documented by the slaves experiencing them. Former slave John Brown described how his master, Dr. Thomas Hamilton of Georgia, performed homemade medical experiments on him in which he was made to sit naked on a stool that rested above a burning pit. As a slave, Brown could not disobey his master, so he had to suffer through whatever Dr. Hamilton subjected him to. Brown said of this experience, "I could not have helped myself. There was nothing for it but passive resignation, and I gave myself up in ignorance and in much fear."[18]

After the temperature of the stool reached 100 degrees, Brown passed out while Dr. Hamilton stood by with a thermometer. Unfortunately for Brown, this was not the only time he would have to endure Dr. Hamilton's curiosity. In another experiment, Dr. Hamilton attempted to determine the width of a black person's skin. He did this by burning and blistering Brown's hands and feet and measuring them after he was injured.

Dr. Hamilton was not unique in subjecting slaves to unnecessary injuries. Hospitals regularly advertised within local communities seeking slaves for participation in experiments. For example, in the 1850s, Dr. T. Stillman sought "sick negroes" who could not adequately perform their daily duties. He wanted to perform experiments that would possibly "heal" the slaves so they could get back to work. Slave owners willingly delivered their slaves to Dr. Stillman in hopes that they would return to productivity. Some did, but others died while participating in the experiments.

Experimentation on African Americans occurred not only during slavery, but well into the 1970s. Until that time, prisons regularly conducted experiments on prisoners without their knowledge or permission, most of whom were black. Dow Chemical Co. paid Philadelphia's Holmesburg prison to test potential carcinogens on the mostly black prison population. The results of the experiments were that many of the prisoners developed certain cancers, skin conditions, and mental illness.

One of the most well-known mass medical experiments on African Americans was the Tuskegee Syphilis Experiment. The Tuskegee Syphilis Experiment was a clinical study conducted between 1932 and 1972 by the U.S. Public Health Service. Its purpose was to study the natural progression of untreated syphilis in African American men. The experiments took place in rural Alabama. To entice participants, the leaders of the experiment told locals that they would be receiving free health care paid for by the federal government. Altogether, 600 black sharecroppers took part in the study. None of the participants knew what was taking place.

When the experiment began, 399 participants were already infected with the disease, while 201 were not infected. During the experiments duration, the participants were provided with free medical care and meals. An extra incentive for participants was a free policy for burial insurance. Funding for the experiment was limited and eventually ran out. This did not deter those conducting it from continuing. The experiment continued, even though none of the participants were advised that it had officially been discontinued. Participants also were not told that they were infected with Syphilis or that they were not receiving proper treatment for their conditions. Although penicillin was available and affordable to those who were conducting the experiment, participants remained untreated and languished from their infections.

In the end, several participants succumbed to their infection, at least 40 women contracted the disease from participants, and 19 children were born with congenital syphilis. The only reason the experiments ended was because a whistleblower eventually advised the government that the experiments had continued, even after the loss of funding. Fortunately, this led to new regulations and protections for people who participate in medical testing, including requiring medical teams to get informed consent from participants, the right for patients to receive clear communication concerning any diagnosis, and accurate reporting of test results for those who participate in experiments or clinical trials. But none of that helped the original subjects.[19]

Legal Support of Racial Division

Slavery is one of America's most grievous enduring legacies. It served as the foundation for much of the country's advancement, and it continues to serve as the foundation for much of the tension felt between black and white. It will continue to affect future generations as well. Ira Glasser wrote, "The residue of slavery and centuries of legal discrimination still stain every institution in this society, and substantially limit the opportunity of many, perhaps most, black children."[20]

The practice of enslaving one race was one of the clearest signs that our founding fathers did not consider black people fully human. Many black men and women, assisted by kind-hearted whites, gave their lives to fight against the institution of slavery—not just for their own sakes, but for the sake of future generations. Christopher Carter wrote, "It is important for blacks to be considered fully human: Being referred to and looked upon as fully human is something black people have fought and died trying to achieve—for my people, our common humanity matters."[21] Although the process of freeing slaves was in full swing in the 1800s, it would be many more years before African Americans were viewed as truly free or even somewhat equal to others. The following are just a few factors that contributed to the delay in African Americans reaching legal equality with whites.

The Dred Scott Decision

Dred Scott was a slave, who, after being moved from a state that supported slavery to a state that did not, attempted to sue his owner in court to gain freedom for himself and his family. Although Scott's effort was valiant, the courts ultimately denied his request for freedom and ordered him to be returned to his owner. In the official ruling against him, the courts determined that, according to the Constitution, any person that was descended from Africans, whether slave or free, was not a citizen of the United States.

The court effectively determined that African Americans had no legal claim to freedom or citizenship, at all. The ruling also determined the following findings:

- Since they were not citizens, African Americans did not possess the legal standing to bring a lawsuit in a federal court.
- Since slaves were private property, Congress did not have the power to regulate slavery in the territories and could not revoke a slave owner's rights based on where he lived.
- This decision nullified the essence of the Missouri Compromise, which divided territories into jurisdictions, either free or slave.
- Because Scott was considered the private property of his owners, he was subject to the Fifth Amendment to

the United States Constitution, which prohibited the taking of property from its owner without due process.

The court determined that, according to the Constitution, slaves really were no more than property and their owners could do with them as they pleased.

Black Codes of the South

Due to the lenient political policies of President Andrew Johnson, white southerners were able to reestablish civil authority in the former Confederate states in 1865 and 1866. They immediately instituted a series of restrictive laws known as "black codes."[22] All-white police departments and militias made up of former Confederate soldiers were tasked with enforcing the codes. The codes were designed to severely restrict the movement of freed African Americans while in certain areas to guarantee their continued availability as a labor force, even though slavery had been abolished. This was exhibited through multiple state and local actions, such as:

- Some states required blacks to sign a yearly labor contract and to produce said contract at a moment's notice when they were asked for it by a white person. If a black person refused to sign a yearly contract, they risked being arrested as vagrants and paying a heavy fine or being forced into unpaid labor.
- Some states enacted laws that prohibited blacks from holding any occupation other than farmer or servant unless they paid an annual tax of $10 to $100.
- Several states passed repressive labor contract laws to dissuade and punish anyone who dared offer black workers higher wages than they were already earning.
- African Americans who violated labor contracts were subject to arrest, beating, and forced labor.
- The apprenticeship laws of many states forced black minors into unpaid positions as laborers for white farmers if they were orphans or if a judge determined their parents were unable to provide adequate support for them.

Convict Leasing

The Thirteenth Amendment to the Constitution effectively made chattel slavery illegal within the United States. In full, the amendment states:

> Neither slavery nor involuntary servitude, except as a punishment for crime whereof the party shall have been duly convicted, shall exist within the United States, or any place subject to their jurisdiction. Congress shall have power to enforce this article by appropriate legislation.[23]

Slaveholders and those who benefited from the practice of slavery were not happy with this development and became obsessed with trying to figure out ways to return blacks to lives of servitude. They found a way to do this via a loophole in the amendment.

The loophole was found in the statement "except as a punishment for crime whereof the party shall have been duly convicted." This made it possible for a black person to be returned to slavery via arrest and conviction for even the pettiest crimes. When this was added to the fact that African Americans already had limited protections against unfair arrest, they were left defenseless against local communities and systems that were not happy that traditional legal slavery had come to an end.

Foreshadowing much of the modern racial profiling and unfair incarceration practices that still happen today, convict leasing was a system of penal labor practiced primarily in the South. It provided prisoner labor to private parties, such as plantation owners and corporations. Through the process, an African American would be arrested and convicted of a crime. After conviction, that person would be leased out to a company or plantation owner and forced to work as slave labor until their debt to society was paid. As you can imagine, no one ever sufficiently worked enough to pay off their societal debt. The state of Louisiana leased out convicts as early as 1844, but the system expanded all through the South with the emancipation of slaves at the end of the Civil War in 1865.

Convict leasing was a way to regularly arrest freed slaves and return them to their former masters at a profit for the State. Under the convict leasing system, the lessee was responsible for feeding, clothing, and housing the prisoners. The person being leased was responsible for doing as they were told or risk the possibility of severe punishment or death. The system was financially lucrative for the states involved. For example, in 1898 73 percent of Alabama's entire annual state revenue came from convict leasing.

Historian Alex Lichtenstein notes that, although Northern states also had a convict leasing system in place, it was in no way as harsh or all-encompassing as that in the South. "Only in the South did the state entirely give up its control of the convict population to the contractor; and only in the South did the physical 'penitentiary' become virtually synonymous with the various private enterprises in which convicts labored."[24] Obviously, this ensured that life would continue to be hard for African Americans. "Corruption, lack of accountability, and racial violence resulted in one of the harshest and most exploitative labor systems known in American history. African Americans, mostly adult males, due to vigorous and selective enforcement of laws and discriminatory sentencing, made up the vast majority—but not all—of the convicts leased."[25]

Jim Crow Laws

Jim Crow Laws were state and local laws that enforced racial segregation throughout the United States after Reconstruction until 1965. The laws covered almost every aspect of potential interaction between white and black people. Some of the most recognizable laws were that it was illegal for African Americans to use white bathrooms or water fountains. Another recognizable law was that while riding on public transportation, a black person had to immediately give up their seat to a white person if asked, and move to the back of the vehicle.

Even after Jim Crow was abolished, in 1967 Richard and Mildred Loving, an interracial couple, were charged under the Virginia Legal Code for violating the law that prohibited interracial couples from being married out of state and then returning to live in Virginia as a married couple. They were also charged with a felony for being an interracial couple. The presiding judge, Leon Bazile, found them guilty of both charges, stating, "Almighty God created the races white, black, yellow, Malay and red, and he placed them on separate continents. And but for the interference with his arrangement there would be no cause for such marriages. The fact that he separated the races shows that he did not intend for the races to mix."[26] The Supreme Court eventually overruled Judge Bazile's decision in the landmark Loving vs. Virginia court case, effectively making any such exclusionary laws invalid. Yet the news apparently did not reach all our states, because it was not until 2000 that, finally, Alabama changed its marriage laws to reflect the Supreme Court decision—the last state to do so.

Nixon Initiatives

The twentieth-century's original "law and order" President, Nixon is remembered for the comments, "We must declare and win the war against the criminal elements which increasingly threaten our cities, our homes and our lives," from the 1970 State of the Union Address. President Richard Nixon laid the groundwork for reinstituting some of the racially tinged practices of law enforcement that had previously been outlawed. President Nixon advocated for higher conviction rates. Nixon put the taxpayer's money where his mouth was between 1969 and 1973 by tripling the federal government's law enforcement budget and increasing federal aid to state and local law enforcement agencies from $60 million to nearly $800 million.[27] Unfortunately, much of law enforcement's efforts at reducing crime were targeted at poor and minority communities.

However, Nixon's efforts did not stop there. During his tenure as president, the Law Enforcement Assistance Administration was born. LEAA was a federal agency within the U.S. Dept. of Justice that administered federal funding to state and local law enforcement agencies and funded educational programs, research, state planning agencies, and local crime initiatives. The significance of LEAA's programs is that much of the resources provided by LEAA were used by agencies and departments to specifically target poor and minority communities. The legislation that gave birth to LEAA also enabled corporations to reintroduce prison labor.

Reagan Initiatives

President Ronald Reagan famously started our nation's "war on drugs" in 1986. Shortly thereafter, the Anti-Drug Abuse Act of 1986 was passed as the crowning achievement of this initiative. Although the act was conceived to help people, it ended up being punitive instead of restorative. Among other things, the law changed the system, negatively affecting minority cultures and changing federal sentencing guidelines.

The changes brought more disparity in how crimes were classified and the punishments that followed. Drug possession for crack cocaine, for instance, became a greater crime with a harsher sentence than for powder cocaine. One is considered a "black drug," the other white, but the primary differences are in how it is processed, the hard "crack" form being cheaper than powder. The original sentencing guidelines had a 100:1 weight ratio disparity between punishment for possession of black drugs versus white drugs. Recently the disparity was changed to 18:1, but black drug convictions still receive longer sentences.[28]

In addition to taking on drugs, Reagan was famous for promoting the "black welfare queen" image in America. Historian Duchess Harris wrote, "The welfare queen is the defining social stereotype of the Black woman, a lazy, promiscuous single Black mother living off the dole of society. She poses a threat to the Protestant work ethic that drives America and the American dream of social advancement and acceptability."[29] This sentiment was echoed by James Kilgore, in his book *Understanding Mass Incarceration*. Mr. Kilgore says, "Creating the image of the Welfare Queen as a criminal misuser of taxpayer dollars and perpetuator of sexual immorality helped build the case for reallocating money from social services to law and order."[30]

In addition to black women becoming the poster children for welfare reform, black men became the poster children for criminal justice reform. This was most evidenced by the portrayal of convicted criminal Willie Horton. Horton was a convicted felon who, while already serving a life sentence for murder without the possibility of parole, was allowed to participate in a weekend furlough program in Massachusetts where presidential candidate Michael Dukakis served as governor. During the furlough period, Willie Horton committed another string of crimes, including raping a white woman.

Horton and his crimes became the centerpiece of a racially based scare campaign for presidential candidate George H.W. Bush. Dennis Rome, a professor of criminal justice, wrote that due to the tactics used by candidate Bush, "Blacks are the repository for the American fear of crime. Ask anyone, of any race, to picture a criminal, and the image will have a black face. The link between blackness and criminality is routinized by terms such as 'black on black crime' and 'black crime.'"[31] Although public discourse of "black on black" crime is common, there is little talk about "white on white" crime, even though a 2011 report from the Department of Justice said that 84 percent of homicides of whites is by whites.[32]

Biased Media Portrayals

In the book *The Black Image in the White Mind*, authors Robert M. Entman and Andrew Rojecki offer a comprehensive look at the subtle patterns of the portrayal of different races and people groups within mass media. They also discuss how these portrayals play a significant role in shaping the attitudes of whites toward blacks. Within the book they show that, typically, whites learn about blacks not through personal relationships but through the images shown by the media. Additionally, they show how media is used to subtly build a pattern that communicates a racial hierarchy in which whites are on top, as well as promoting a sense of difference and conflict between the two groups.[33]

The authors also shed light on how television news programs focus on black poverty and crime disproportionately in portrayals of black life. Many media outlets have used black experts only for limited black-themed issues, while distorting black politics. The authors conclude that though there are more images of African Americans on television now than ever, these images are often harmful to race relations.

Some specific findings show that mug shots of a black defendant are four times more likely to appear in local television news reports than those of a white defendant. When a black person is accused of a crime, they are twice as likely to be shown physically restrained than whites. And, the name of the accused is twice as likely to be shown on screen if the defendant is black.

Their research also revealed that Black actors are now more visible in films, but black women were shown using profanity and being physically violent far more than white females. And black female characters were shown being restrained 55% of the time, while white female characters were shown being restrained only 6% of the time.

We must pay attention to this because there are consequences. What is seen on television not only influences children and other consumers, but also law enforcement. "The media perpetuate ideas linking race with criminality... The prevalent typification of Blacks as criminals seems to justify law enforcement tactics that exploit race in criminal investigations."[34]

Biased Bible-Teaching and Christian Belief

One of the primary false doctrines that emerged from white ideology into theology is the supposed "Curse of Ham" doctrine. Founded on the misinterpretation of Genesis 9:20–27, it served as one of the primary validations for enslaving people unfortunate enough to be born with black skin. In that passage, Ham finds his father Noah drunk and naked in a tent. Ham tells his brothers, Shem and Japheth, about their father's condition. Shem and Japheth quickly act to cover their father's body without accidentally looking at his nakedness. When Noah sobers up and realizes what happened, he announces a curse on Ham's son Canaan. The curse was that Canaan would be "a servant of servants" (NKJV).

As the slave trading industry began to boom, the "curse of Ham" represented Africans and their descendants, the "sons of Ham," and their black skin was the sign of the curse. This idea excused whites from feeling any shame for enslaving them, since they were cursed to live as servants anyway. One of the ironies about the curse of Ham is that neither Noah or any of his family were ever described as black, white, or any other race.

Paul's letter to Philemon also served those who supported enslavement of black people. Paul's words encouraging the slave Onesimus to return to his master Philemon were used to justify slavery and encourage slaves to stay with their masters in contemporary times. Using the letter, slave masters could tell their slaves that God did not want them free in the here and now, but freedom would be available in the afterlife.

Slave masters were primarily concerned about keeping their slaves in fear so they would perform their duties without hesitation. They were not concerned about their slave's souls, only the health of their bodies so they could work. Authors Michael Emerson and Christian Smith write, "Traditionally, white Christians paid little attention to slaves' souls. The pre-1700 views that black slaves were less than fully human, did not possess souls, and were incapable of learning, as well as simple indifference by white Christians all led to a lack of interest in proselytizing slaves."[35]

Over time, "Christianizing" slaves came to be viewed as a Christian responsibility. But, the push to convert slaves was not embraced by the public. Objections to proselytizing blacks ranged from the older notion that Africans did not have eternal souls, to the idea that blacks were incapable of learning the Christian faith. The true reason was certain people wanted to maintain the social order that benefitted them. If slaves became Christians it would mean equality, freedom, or slave revolts. The fear of this stemmed from an unwritten rule in some white churches that said if a slave accepted Christ and was baptized, they were not only freed from sin, but also slavery. Certain clergy members quickly worked to fight against this custom, initially arguing that Christian freedom did not free slaves from the temporal bondage of this world.

Beginning as early as 1644, certain clergy encouraged colonial legislators to declare that slaves should remain slaves, even after baptism. They encouraged Anglican Bishop George Berkeley to request a formal statement from Britain's Attorney General and Solicitor General. Both men determined that baptism did not reverse or nullify slave status within the British Kingdom. In 1727, Anglican Bishop Edmund Gibson declared:

> Christianity, and the embracing of the gospel, does not make the least alteration in civil property, or in any duties which belong to civil relations: but in all these respects, it continues persons just in the same state as it found them. The freedom which Christianity gives, is a freedom from the bondage of sin and Satan, and from the dominion of men's lusts and passions and inordinate desires; but as to their outward condition, whatever that was before, whether bond or free, their being baptized, and becoming Christians makes no matter of change in it.[36]

Rev. Cotton Mather forcefully argued that the Bible did not give Christian slaves the right to liberty and freedom. He also argued that neither the teachings of the church, nor the English constitution, made a connection between becoming a Christian and experiencing freedom from slavery. Instead, slavery was an advantageous institution for all involved.

However, not all clergy who believed this were sufficiently convinced that it would be easy keeping converted slaves in their place. These clergy members sought ways to continue to convince slaves that it was more beneficial and Christlike for them to remain submissive. One way to do this was to make slaves adhere to certain vows at baptism. One such vow read in part, "You declare in the presence of God and before this congregation that you do not ask for the holy baptism out of any design to free yourself from the Duty and Obedience you owe to your Master while you live, but merely for the good of Your soul and to partake of the Graces and Blessings promised to the Members of the Church of Jesus Christ."[37]

Other clergy members took more drastic and dastardly steps to keep slaves in line. In their minds, not only did Christianity make slaves better slaves, it also did not hinder owners from using whatever means necessary to obtain obedient compliance from those slaves. When Bishop Gibson wrote on the issue, he declared that if a slave behaved badly, Christianity did not remove from masters the use of any method they deemed necessary to enforce obedience from slaves. Whether slaves were baptized or not, owners had the authority to determine the necessary punishment in instances of the slightest insubordination.

Peter's Predicament

Now, let's return to the cafeteria, where Peter's friends are questioning and berating him. "You willingly ate with someone from McGregor?" the debate captain snarls. "You ignored the rules!"

Peter stays calm and begins to recount his soon-to-be-infamous excuse. "I know. But, while I was in Waco, I had a vision. Not an ordinary vision, but something off the charts. A big sheet floated down from the sky with all kinds of animals on it—pigs, birds, and snakes. And God told me to kill and eat them.

"'But God,' I said. 'I follow the rules; I can't make my body unclean.' God told me, 'What I've made clean, do not call unclean.' This happened not once, not twice, but three times. And, after the third time, the sheet floated back up into the sky.

"Now, you won't believe this, but three guys came, big McGregor Bulldogs, and told me a man had seen an angel who told him that I would be in Waco, and they should come find me because I would tell them how they could be saved."

"Yeah, right," the debate captain says as the rest of the team crowds in behind to listen. Then, someone asks what happened next, and Peter knows he's got them hooked.

"Then, the strangest thing of all happened," he continues. "As I talked to these big guys, they were suddenly overcome like drunk men, filled with a holy fire. I thought we were the only ones who could experience God like that, but, as I watched them, it dawned on me: God was bringing them in, and making them a part of God's family. And, if God was willing to do that for them, who was I to stand in their way?"

The entire cafeteria is silent, everyone sitting stunned. Mouths are open in shock. No one even attempts to debate. What Peter has said begins to sink in, and they eventually sit up straight and begin to celebrate. They realize God has granted salvation and new life to those they thought were unable to be saved. Once their hated football rivals, now their brothers in Christ. Everything would have to change.

Yes, even the fledgling church struggled with racial division and its implications. Jesus' followers had to overcome the prejudice that Gentiles were not a part of the Jewish lineage and did not fit their preferences or expectations. Could they even be saved and join their group? How? Their background was so different, could they be considered fully equal as members of God's family?

Up to that point, one of the ways of showing who was in or who was out of a group was whether you were willing to spend time with them over a meal. Some people referred to it as having "table fellowship." A Jewish person could not eat with a Gentile, especially in a Gentile's home, unless they wanted to become unclean and be outside of fellowship with God.

However, Peter—and the six men who went with him— voluntarily became "unclean." And, they did not apologize for it, and did not ask questions. They went to see what God would do. And God eventually did something wonderful.

What they learned was that Gentiles could be true Jesus followers without adopting Jewish customs or having a certain pedigree. They did not have to follow the laws or restrictions. In Acts 10, Cornelius, the Gentile who almost causes Peter to be ostracized, is said to be a man who simply fears God and does good things for other people. If that sounds familiar, it should: Jesus said the summation of the law was to Love God and love your neighbor. And without a lot of hoopla, Cornelius follows the example of Jesus and his family are eventually welcomed into the family of God.

This serves as a marker for a new understanding of God. All people are now ceremonially clean in God's eyes, worthy to be a part of God's family. It seems God is turning everything the early church thought they knew on its ear.

So, how did you feel when people "put you in a box," or relegated you to a specific table? Did they think they had the right to tell you who you were and where they thought you belonged? Did they know you? Or, did they only think they did?

Why do so many people never move on from those boxes, even as adults? We no longer sit at lunch room tables, but we still separate ourselves by social groups, by where we live, by our economic status, and especially by the color of our skin. We've been taught well by other people throughout our entire lives. And, whether it was scientists influencing us with shoddy data about a certain "intellectual inferiority," or media portrayals of certain people as "criminals" or especially violent, or interpretations of the Bible that say certain people are cursed by God—to combat these faulty ideas, we must intentionally seek to learn about those certain people who are so different from us.

Are they so different, after all?

Think about someone who does not fit at your "table." How might you invite them to spend some time with you? Can you leave your table to simply get to know them, their history, their family, their dreams? How clearly would we reflect God's love if we regularly did this?

2

The Normality of Whiteness

"The most important issue in understanding racism is not what it does to *hurt* people of color, but what it does to *help* white people. "

—JOSEPH BARNDT[1]

A primary reason for the continued existence of much racial tension and separation in the twenty-first century is the normality of whiteness and the perceived abnormality of other skin colors. "The subtle racism of twenty-first century America is 'civilizational racism,' a mindset that assumes whiteness to be normative and superior."[2] Most people believe what stems from white assumptions, culture, needs, and thinking should be given priority over and against the needs and preferences of all minority cultures, and all minority cultures should conform to whiteness and its dominance.

The idea of whiteness as the standard influences every aspect of American life:

The power of white-as-normal is so common that it regulates social and political structures, often without participants recognizing they are its willing disciples. White-as-normal shapes what is believed to be civilized behavior. Historical depictions of Jesus

43

and of God as white render this regulating practice as sacred, giving religious justification to the normative role of whiteness. [3]

It even influences minority cultures to try to modify their natural physical characteristics:

> Beauty, intelligence, piety and every other mark of personhood are indexed along a spectrum of whiteness. For example, nonwhite persons who want to be seen (by themselves and others) as physically attractive have to come up with ways to look white. In the 19th and 20th centuries a veritable industry emerged to supply the cosmetic techniques (from methods for hair straightening to skin lighteners to plastic surgery) for this passage into whiteness.[4]

This also includes deferring to white preferences in all major areas of life, including language used, beliefs espoused, and actions considered acceptable in public:

> The subtle and sometimes unconscious ideology of white superiority is the fundamental problem in American race relations. White superiority is a system in which 'white' bodies, and cultural and social practices associated with those deemed 'white'—are seen as normative and superior, and through which white people are granted advantaged status of various kinds.[5]

Some whites don't see the normality of whiteness. They don't think they are better than anyone else. They don't necessarily put their desires ahead of those of other races. But, one of the benefits of normative whiteness is you don't even have to think about it. "Whites who talk with me about White supremacy need to be informed and sensitive to the common humanity we all share. All I ask of Whites is to put themselves in Black people's place in this society and the world, and then ask themselves what they would say or do if they were in Black people's place."[6]

Where Did Whiteness as the Standard Come From?

The normality of whiteness is not only important to discussions of politics and economic equality. It is important to how we view and live the Christian faith and understand its theology. Consider: Who are the preferred, celebrated, and trusted voices of classic and contemporary Christian faith? What point of view is Christian theology studied from? The answer to those questions is the white perspective—and, more specifically, the white *male* perspective.

What do those from non-white male backgrounds have to do to be considered legitimate in the world of Christian theology? They must conform to the views of the dominant culture, speak the theological language of the dominant culture, and wait their turn for participation in certain sectors of contemporary Christian theology—because, there cannot be too many minority faces and voices vying for attention at one time.

Whiteness as the standard is unrepresentative of God and God's desires—in many ways. The assumption does not recognize God has created all people equally, regardless of ethnicity or skin color. It does not recognize God speaks through all types of people equally. It also does not recognize various people groups have diverse experiences, which can affect their understanding of scripture and God's actions in the world. For example, historically, African Americans have viewed the Exodus narratives through the lens of those longing for freedom from their oppressors, while whites have been able to primarily spiritualize the book.

This practice of whiteness as the norm has served as the foundation for American church life for centuries and, typically, has not been perceived as negative. It is a part of our nature to think this way. We are taught to accept it without even questioning or recognizing its prevalence in our lives. When confronted with it, some whites will defend themselves by saying they don't see color. Again, this is one of the primary benefits of being white. "The proclivity of whites to disregard our own racial characteristics may be a defining characteristic of whiteness: to be white is not to think about it."[7]

How are we to address this with the hope of improving race relations in our nation? The first step is recognizing that a white standard is the foundation for how our nation operates. As Ian Haney López points out in *White by Law,* we crucially need to undergo a paradigm shift—away from assuming whites are innocent and superior and live in a "nonracist society," toward being aware of a pervasive, largely unconscious racism within our society specifically intended to protect white privilege and cultural hegemony.[8]

And as Dr. Willie James Jennings said in an article entitled "Overcoming Racial Faith": "We repeat the mistake continuously in this country of trying to address our racial animus and the violence it fosters as though it were a virus that occasionally attacks our social body, rather than seeing the truth: that racial animus is a constituting reality of our social body."[9]

He adds:

> Our racial struggles are intractable, because we refuse to see how deeply their roots are embedded in the ways we think, live, and imagine the world socially. Race in America is a form of religious faith, and we will never be able to understand or address it with the necessary knowledge, energy, or commitment until we comprehend its true architecture. Indeed, race has a Christian architecture, and Christianity in the West has a racial architecture.[10]

To Dr. Jennings, the origins of the white standard are obvious. We inherited "tropes" of white as good, and black as evil, from early European culture and language. In the original colonies, *white* and *black* became embedded as theological symbols—as a way of seeing truth versus lie, goodness versus bad, and beauty versus scum:

> Whiteness emerged as the ground for the universal, by which I mean the ability of the one to represent the many as well as the ability of the one to present reality

on behalf of the many. White bodies were established as normative humanity in all its majesty or weakness. Whiteness emerged out of Christianity and unleashed a power that remains difficult to comprehend—unless one understands that Christianity always invokes comprehensive vision. Anyone and everyone may be seen through the lens of sinner and saved, faithful or faithless.[11]

Whiteness in the West, he says, has become "not a particular person, not a particular gender, not a particular nation, but an invitation, a becoming, a transformation, an accomplishment."[12] In the new world, the founders chose to establish a world free of considering the lens of different peoples.

One of the earliest ways whiteness was established as the standard in the United States was through the concept of manifest destiny, "the belief or doctrine, held chiefly in the middle and latter part of the 19th century, that it was the destiny of the U.S. to expand its territory over the whole of North America and to extend and enhance its political, social, and economic influences."[13] This was evidenced by the early settlers' intentional expansion from east to west coasts. They traveled across the new land with little regard for who or what they encountered, or how their expansion would affect land, animals, and natural resources.

They viewed expansion as a righteous, religious act to obey. Dr. Jennings states, "European Christians saw themselves as the bearers of the true faith and therefore as destined by God to be the teachers of the world."[14] This was possible because there existed "a racist sense of manifest destiny by which white Christians in the United States were recognized as God's chosen people, divinely selected to dominate the earth."[15]

James Cone agrees:

Can any nation discover what belonged to someone else?" asked the seventeenth-century Dutch Jurist Hugo Grotius. Few Europeans asked such questions, but instead, exploited lands and peoples unhindered by philosophy, religion or ethics. In fact, these disciplines assisted them in justifying their violence as they viewed themselves as God's chosen people to subdue the indigenous people and their land. [16]

Dr. Cone continues:

Through cultural and religious imperialism, Europeans imposed their racist value-system on people of color and thereby forced them to think that the only way to be human and civilized was to be White and Christian. It not only makes the oppressed want to be something other than they are but also to become like their oppressors. Malcolm X called it self-hate—the worst mental sickness imaginable.[17]

It was possible for whites to treat blacks, and people of other nationalities, in the ways outlined in chapter one of this book because whites did not view non-whites as fully human. White forefathers determined black bodies were not fully human. "Indeed, the plurality of white American Christianity sanctioned the notion that black bodies were initially less human than their own, and ultimately needed to be defined against a white ideal. In this sense, the track record of white American Christianity's valuation of black bodies is at best unsettling."[18]

This is not new information. Our nation and its guiding principles were developed by and for white men, the majority of whom did not view Africans or their descendants as equal to them. As I previously stated, our nation's legal, medical, and social systems were developed, not to benefit black people, but to instead cause them to live as subordinates to others. And, our nation's historic racism toward black people is not unique. Multiple examples exist of prior nations and civilizations that ostracized blacks solely due to their skin color.

Around 2,000 b.c.e., the following was chiseled into a granite stele near a boundary between Egypt and Nubia, expressing the Egyptians' disdain for those of darker skin color (unless their interactions were based on business):

> No Black man whatsoever shall be permitted to pass this place going down stream (the Nile) no matter whether he is travelling by desert or journeying in a boat—except such Blacks as come to do business in the country or travelling on an embassy. Such, however, shall be well treated in every way whatsoever. But no boats belonging to Blacks, shall in the future be permitted to pass down this river.[19]

Although Egyptians may have had problems with people with darker skin, early Hebrews evidently did not. Some point to the intermarriage of Moses to the Cushite woman Zipporah as evidence. Consider what Gayraud Wilmore offers in this vein:

> Some people evidently assigned a pejorative meaning to blackness long before the beginning of African slavery—for whatever reason—and if the Bible itself seems relatively free of this prejudice it is only because the Jews (Hebrews), after many years of residence and intermarriage in Africa, were themselves a dark-skinned people by the time the Old Testament had been written.[20]

Over time, however, Hebrews too began to have disdain for those with darker skin:

> Victims of prejudice themselves, the Medieval Jews simply consigned black people to a lower status than themselves. It was not the Jews of the Old Testament period, but Jews and Gentiles of medieval Europe—especially of Northern Europe and Great Britain—who were repelled by black skin color and African physiogamy and gave renewed vigor to the color prejudice that had been sporadic and peripheral in the ancient world.[21]

Other nations followed suit. As Frank Snowden relates:

[In Greco-Roman culture] there was a belief in certain circles that the color of the Ethiopian's skin was ominous, related no doubt to the association of the color black with death, the underworld, and evil. It was noted, for example, among omens presaging disaster that ill-starred persons were known to have seen an Ethiopian before their misfortune. An Ethiopian who met the troops of Cassius and Brutus as they were proceeding to battle was considered an omen of disaster. Among the events listed as foreshadowing the death of Septimius Severas was his encounter with an Ethiopian. [22]

This erroneous thinking was carried from Egypt and Europe to the new world. Early settlers used the Bible to support their arguments that the white race was the only race that could be considered fully human and blessed with full personhood.

The Bible and Christianity as Tools of Whiteness

The Bible and Christian theology were used to confirm the ethnicity of God:

But the dychotomy [*sic*] of whiteness and blackness, and the imputation of positive value to the former and negative value to the latter, is deeply etched into the consciousness of the white people of Europe and America. Rather than something "unnatural" and peripheral to Western civilization it is of the essence of this civilization and, in modern times, has been elevated almost to the status of an ontological reality. God himself is white for Western man and the Christian faith, inextricably bound in its development to the history and culture of the great Western powers, is a white religion—a religion of, by and for white people. That is not a fantastic idea concocted by fanatical African priests and storefront preachers to persuade their people to resist white domination. It is not some wild allegation dreamed up by the

Rastafarians or the Black Muslims. It just happens to
be the simple, unadorned truth about what has been
given to Black people as Christianity and something
white people themselves believed.[23]

Christian theology became one of the primary tools to
separate the races and relegate blacks to a lower position
of physical, spiritual, and theological servanthood. "In the
worst of times, classic theological texts have been used to
oppress persons of color and women. In the best of times,
the overwhelming attention given these particular voices
obscured other voices, giving the impression that the only
Christians speaking and writing about God for the last 2,000
years were European men."[24] The white theological response
to this type of pushback from black theologians was swift
and pointed. "When black theology championed the black
church as the location of God's preference and accused white
Christianity of heresy, white theologians only saw secularism
run amok. Or at least they could claim as much, allowing
them to dismiss much black theology outright no matter how
scripturally anchored it was."[25]

As contemporary theology grew, so did the desire to
further clarify the perceived distinction between blacks and
whites and God's view of each group:

Under the influence of Calvinism and later Puritanism,
however, the notion of election became secularized to
mean economic and material success. The whiteness
or blackness of the skin accordingly came to have a
secular meaning also. Thus, whiteness of skin came
to symbolize material, scientific and technological
successes while blackness of skin came to be equated
with a prescientific mentality, with economic poverty
and with ignorance.[26]

Dennis Hoekstra illustrates this point further, stating:

Racial ideologizing takes place when a group of
people of one race wants to think about or treat
those of other races as being inferior, and then builds

a Biblio-theological basis to support this position. Through racial ideologizing our Dutch Reformed forefathers could support a lucrative slave trade and slavery in their colonies and justify to themselves the awful evils of these practices. They maintained that God made Negroes the slaves of whites through the curse upon Ham and Canaan recorded in Genesis 9. It is now clear that reputable Biblical exegesis and even a cursory knowledge of geography and history make this view untenable. Yet this did not stop our well-educated and Biblically oriented Dutch Calvinist predecessors from maintaining for centuries, and perhaps even creating, as DeLubac suggests, a Biblically based ideology to support racial discrimination.[27]

Personhood in the Bible

So what does the Bible teach about personhood as it relates to race? In general, it does not specifically address the question of who is qualified to have personhood, but it does tell us what it means to be human and to have traits that make us different from the other parts of creation—such as animals, angels, etc. It does tell us that human beings were created in the image and likeness of God, and they have similar emotional traits, the ability to solve problems, create things, and communicate complex ideas—primary elements of personhood.

In the book *The New Testament World: Insights from Cultural Anthropology*, author Bruce J. Malina says, "Personhood is expressed by how we relate to God and community."[28] According to Malina, people living during Bible times were particularly group-oriented, especially racial/ethnic oriented, and believed this defined who they were. "Your identity...included those with the same ethnic heritage and mutual acquaintances. Those within the in-group can [sic] have interpersonal relationships with one another, but those outside would be treated impersonally. People did not see themselves as individuals, but as part of the group, and that they had no identity apart from their group."[29]

Personhood was tied to how well you represented your community. The ultimate concern of personhood was to protect the reputation of a community. David May says,

> Honor [was] analogous to contemporary society's credit rating. If a person's credit rating is high, then he or she receives more goods, incurs more credit, moves in different social circles and receives social recognition. Shame/honor was implicit in every interaction undertaken in the first century world. The ultimate concern for a person living in the first century was his or her honor rating.[30]

American settlers used the biblical idea of honor to deny basic rights to Africans. Pilgrims viewed blacks as godless heathens and animals, intrinsically not worthy of honor. Blacks came from the cursed lineage of Ham, therefore their only identity could be shame-based, as property to be bought and sold.

And, honor was not the only thing unavailable to blacks. They would also miss out on heaven. A reverend of the time said, "Now as Adam was white, Abraham white and our Savior white, did he enter heaven when he arose from the dead as a white man or as a negro?... How could our Savior 'being in the express image of God's person,' as asserted by St. Paul, carry such a damned color into heaven, where all are white, much less to the throne?"[31]

All in all, the idea of whiteness as the standard does not necessarily need Christian scripture to make it valid. Its validity is ensured by the fact that whites drive much of the world. As James Baldwin argues:

> The idea of (whiteness as the standard) rests simply on the fact that white men are the creators of civilization (the present civilization, which is the only one that matters; all previous civilizations are simply "contributions" to our own) and are therefore civilization's guardians and defenders. Thus, it was

impossible for Americans to accept the black man as one of themselves, for to do so was to jeopardize their status as white men. But not so to accept him [sic] was to deny his human reality, his human weight and complexity, and the strain of denying the overwhelmingly undeniable forced Americans into rationalizations so fantastic that they approached the pathological.[32]

Although our nation's founding fathers did use Christian scripture as their foundation, their interpretation and application of said scripture was at best corrupted and divisive, and at worst sacrilegious and deadly. Their version of Christianity "introduced a form of modern Christianity that is not open to learning, changing, adapting, and becoming new but that assimilates peoples and/or segregates peoples into their own separate versions of Christianity. This way of thinking is a hallmark of racial faith."[33]

Blacks were not the only ones affected by this. Whites experienced negative spiritual and theological consequences, as well. Edward Huenemann expands on this idea:

Racism is, therefore, not merely a threat to the victims who suffer its injustice. It is a real threat to mature faith for those who do not know how it undercuts their knowledge of Jesus as the Christ. It leaves them with an impersonal rationalized abstraction. It calls them to worship an exclusive, limited, narrowly defined God. It prevents them from knowing and experiencing the presence among us of a God who breaks down barriers by becoming one with those who are excluded.[34]

Where Has Whiteness as the Standard Taken Us?

What do our nation's forefathers have to do with whiteness as the standard in the twenty-first century? They took immense pride in laying the groundwork for a new country. The foundation of that work, again, was their Christian faith—a faith that believed God was with them, directing them, even when they were conquering native people.

"From slavery to segregation, white evangelicals have often been blind to their role in perpetuating racism and often justified it through conservative evangelical theologies."[35] In many ways, the seeds of this mindset have blossomed in this century and produced "appropriate fruit" in the election of Donald Trump as president. Trump, who ran on a platform of making America "great" again, received 81 percent of the evangelical Christian vote.[36] Kristin Du Mez notes:

> Indeed, white evangelical support for Trump can be seen as the culmination of a decades-long embrace of militant masculinity, a masculinity that has enshrined patriarchal authority, condoned a callous display of power at home and abroad, and functioned as a linchpin in the political and social worldviews of conservative white evangelicals. In the end, many evangelicals did not vote for Trump despite their beliefs, but because of them.[37]

The support for Trump crossed economic boundaries within the white community:

> An analysis of exit polls conducted during the presidential primaries estimated the median household income of Trump supporters to be about $72,000. But even this lower number is almost double the median household income of African Americans, and $15,000 above the American median. Trump's white support was not determined by income. According to Edison Research, Trump won whites making less than $50,000 by 20 points, whites making $50,000 to $99,999 by 28 points, and whites making $100,000 or more by 14 points. This shows that Trump assembled a broad white coalition that ran the gamut from Joe the Dishwasher to Joe the Plumber to Joe the Banker. So, when white pundits cast the elevation of Trump as the handiwork of an inscrutable white working class, they are being too modest, declining to

claim credit for their own economic class. Trump's dominance among whites across class lines is of a piece with his larger dominance across nearly every white demographic. Trump won white women (+9) and white men (+31). He won white people with college degrees (+3) and white people without them (+37). He won whites ages 18–29 (+4), 30–44 (+17), 45–64 (+28), and 65 and older (+19). Trump won whites in midwestern Illinois (+11), whites in mid-Atlantic New Jersey (+12), and whites in the Sun Belt's New Mexico (+5). In no state that Edison polled did Trump's white support dip below 40 percent. Hillary Clinton's did, in states as disparate as Florida, Utah, Indiana, and Kentucky. From the beer track to the wine track, from soccer moms to NASCAR dads, Trump's performance among whites was dominant.[38]

In general, a vast number of people who voted for Trump consider themselves evangelical Christians and seek to return America to its "Christian foundation." But, does contemporary evangelical faith help foster whiteness as the standard or does contemporary evangelical faith fight against it? To answer that question, we need to understand a few foundational truths about evangelicalism in the twenty-first century as it relates to the subject of race.

James Cone writes:

Whites do not talk about racism because they do not have to talk about it. They have most of the power in the world—economic, political, social, cultural, intellectual, and religious. There is little that blacks and other people of color can do to change the power relations in the churches, seminaries, and society. Powerful people do not talk, except on their own terms and almost never at the behest of others. All the powerless can do is to disrupt—make life uncomfortable for the ruling elites.[39]

Additionally, Cone states:

White theologians avoid racial dialogue because talk about white supremacy arouses deep feelings of guilt. Guilt is a heavy burden to bear. Most Americans have at least a general idea of the terrible history of white supremacy and that alone can create a profound guilt when blacks and others tell their stories of suffering and pain. Whites know that they have reaped the material harvest of white domination in the modern world.[40]

According to Cone, white evangelicals also avoid race conversations because they believe that blacks will become angry:

Another reason why whites avoid race topics with African Americans is because they do not want to engage black rage. Whites do not mind talking as long as blacks don't get too emotional, too carried away with their stories of hurt. I must admit that it is hard to talk about the legacies of white supremacy and not speak with passion and anger about the long history of black suffering. It is not a pleasant thing to talk about, especially for people of color who have experienced white cruelty. I would not recommend race as a topic of conversation during a relaxed social evening of blacks and whites. Things could get a little heated and spoil a fun evening.[41]

It is understandable that most white evangelicals do not want to bear responsibility for past injustices perpetrated by their forefathers. Cone continues:

Whites do not like to think of themselves as evil people or that their place in the world is due to the colonization of Indians, the enslavement of blacks, and the exploitation of people of color here and around the world. Whites like to think of themselves as hard working, honorable, decent, and fair-minded people. They resent being labeled thieves, murders, slaveholders, and racists. There are whites who say that they do not owe blacks anything because they did not enslave anybody, did not segregate or lynch anybody, and are not white supremacists. They claim to be colorblind and thus treat everybody alike. At an individual level, there is some common sense truth about that observation. But if you benefit from the past and present injustices committed against blacks, you are partly and indirectly accountable as an American citizen and as a member of the institutions that perpetuate racism. We cannot just embrace what is good about America and ignore the bad. We must accept the responsibility to do everything we can to correct America's past and present wrongs.[42]

Despite understanding the feelings whites may have when involved in conversations about race, people of color are still compelled to challenge whites to engage in the discussion. Cone explains:

The quality of white life is hardly ever affected by what blacks think or do...Everything whites think and do impact profoundly the lives of blacks on a daily basis. We can never escape white power and its cruelty. That is why blacks are usually open to talking to whites in the hope of relieving their pain but the latter seldom offer a like response, because they perceive little or nothing to gain.[43]

Sociologists Michael Emerson and Christian Smith have conducted extensive research on the modern-day white evangelical perspective on race, in part through hundreds of interviews with self-identified white evangelicals. Their findings indicate that white evangelicals view the American race problem originating in one or more of the following ways:

- Prejudiced individuals who cause hostility and conflict;
- People of color making racism a group issue or social structural problem;

• A fabrication of self-interest groups—people of color, liberals, the media, or the government.[44]

Emerson summarizes, "White evangelicals generally operate within a 'Ku Klux Klan model of racism,' meaning they understand racism as deliberate and hostile prejudice against people of color perpetrated by a few radical individuals."[45] One of the immediate problems with this view is that it sees racism only as deliberate hostility perpetrated by a few. Yet there are also other problems with this view. "This perpetrator perspective leads many white evangelicals to overlook ordinary racism, such as socioeconomic patterns that disadvantage people of color. Emerson and Smith's research suggests that while most white evangelicals criticize the Ku Klux Klan, few insist that socioeconomic inequality between racial groups is immoral and must be counteracted."[46]

Emerson and Smith later state, "It further indicates that most white evangelicals assume that the vast majority of whites are not racially prejudiced. Thus, when asked about America's race problem, white evangelicals often accuse people of color of exaggerating it."[47] If whites don't think race is an issue that needs to be addressed, there's no problem. African Americans must *choose* to be unhappy by perpetuating an untrue stereotype.

Many evangelicals state that they actively attempt to be color-blind in their interactions with people, meaning they try not to place an emphasis on a person's race during their interactions. Pastor Geoffrey Noel Schoonmaker, who has written about preaching as a beneficial tool in the fight to counteract racism in the church, states:

> In assuming that racism consists of individual attitudes and actions, color-blindness does not account for the social origins of racism. Worse yet, in seeking to remove the significance of race, color-blindness implies the elimination of the distinctive cultures of racial minorities. Color-blindness, therefore, reinforces the dominance of white culture.[48]

In general, white evangelicals say a person's race is not the primary factor that guides their thinking about people. Instead, their thinking is primarily guided by how a person applies the Protestant work ethic to their lives. They typically hold to the ideas of individualism and personal responsibility in life as the primary indicators of a person's success in life. Schoonmaker summarizes the work of sociologist Pamela Perry on this subject, saying, "The values of individualism, personal responsibility, mind over body, self-control, self-determination, and 'the belief that the present holds no debt to the past' are characteristic of white culture, though many assume them to be universally valid."[49]

The following are the general characteristics of 21st-century white evangelical culture:

- *Individualism*–The evangelical emphasis on having a "personal relationship" with Christ through faith, prayer, and Bible reading. Research suggests this can result in privatism and narcissism.
- *Anti-intellectualism*–According to research, there is a widespread assumption in evangelicalism that critical thinking hinders the propagation of the gospel, Christianity's chief task. Mark Noll suggests that a desire to take urgent action leads evangelicals to over-simplify intricate issues rather than engaging in careful, critical reflection.[50]
- *Anti-structuralism*–White evangelicals' emphasis on personal accountability frequently leads them to deny that individual decisions are subject to social structures. Whatever is wrong in people's lives is ascribed to personal responsibility. Emerson's research suggests that white evangelicals often underestimate how legal patterns, institutional patterns, employment patterns, political patterns, and the like influence personal opportunities and choices. It further suggests that white evangelicals are often unwilling to accept explanations of social problems—including racial inequality—based on anything besides individual conduct.[51]

- *Consumerism*–Research suggests that white evangelicals tend to view the church as an institution that caters to their individual needs and spiritual preferences. They often choose the church that best suits their preferences and then change churches whenever another church better suits them.
- *Other-worldly focus*–White evangelicals frequently display "a fascination with heaven while slighting attention to earth, a devotion to the supernatural and a neglect of the natural."[52] "Noll's research indicates that white evangelical focus on the eternal afterlife can undercut attention to racism and other social problems that are viewed as aspects of a transient world."[53]

The general problem with this multi-tiered belief system is it doesn't allow people to see the big picture—structural racism, and the inequality and effects of the system. "Individualism not only blinds white evangelicals to structural inequalities involving race, but it also assigns blame to those who are disadvantaged by race and normalizes and naturalizes cultural practices, beliefs, and norms that privilege white Americans over others."[54]

The white evangelical solution to racism is to convert more people to Christianity. "White evangelicals assume that transforming individuals is the way to rectify social problems. Specifically, many white evangelicals affirm the 'miracle motif,' which states that social problems are automatically solved as more and more people convert to Christianity."[55] That this idea is prevalent among evangelicals was verified through a survey conducted by the University of Akron, which showed that 73 percent of evangelical laypersons agreed with the statement, "If enough people are brought to Christ, social ills will take care of themselves."[56] As one white evangelical told Emerson and Smith, "If everybody was a Christian, there wouldn't be a race problem. We'd all be the same."[57]

According to Emerson and Smith's research, white evangelicals commonly propose the following solutions to racism:

- Become a Christian.
- Love your individual neighbors.
- Establish a cross-race friendship.
- Give individuals the right to pursue jobs and individual justice without discrimination by other individuals.
- Ask forgiveness of individuals one has wronged.

If only life were that easy!

There are multiple drawbacks to these solutions. These solutions do not consider the past or its effect on our current situation. Christianity founded our nation, but it was also used to subjugate people of color, and Christians still struggle to view all races as equal. Another problem is that, typically, when white evangelicals form cross-race relationships, they are with minorities from similar worldviews or levels of affluence. The minority culture may be diminished for the white person, allowing whiteness to remain the dominant standard. Also, diminishing individual injustices does not address the systemic inequalities in American life.

Overall, the white evangelical view of race identified by Emerson and Smith is inadequate to bring about substantial positive change in America for several reasons. Namely, if white evangelicals do not believe there's a race problem, they are not obligated to have a conversation about it. If it can be suggested that a minorities' life problems are due to their laziness or lack of motivation, then there really is no race problem. If evangelicals can believe faith in Christ will fix our race problem, then they can relax and assume everything will eventually be fine. Ultimately, it is not white people's fault that race is such a big problem. It only exists in minorities' minds.

Those statements represent the types of arguments put forth by evangelical Christians when confronted with conversations about racial inequities. Ira Glasser writes:

> School segregation, they will claim, is the result of housing patterns and cannot be blamed on the actions and patterns of school boards. Housing segregation, they will claim, is the result of economic differences, not racial discrimination. And economic differences,

we are told, cannot be traced to employment discrimination or the acts of government, but to lack of education and qualifications. Are racial differentials in education somehow connected to racial discrimination in schools? No, we are told, such differentials are mainly the consequences of broken families. At first glance, each of these arguments by itself has just enough merit to blur the moral clarity of the results. Thus is blame often shifted onto the victims themselves. Detailed scrutiny, however, nearly always reveals certain official acts that were a critical factor in causing such racially disparate results. But it requires a considerable attention span to sustain such scrutiny and more than a minor expenditure of time, effort and money.[58]

Due to certain media and political pressures, there may be a growing realization within the white evangelical church that blacks' complaints about discrimination should be heard, but there is not necessarily a corresponding willingness to tackle the philosophies and theologies that make white people the "ideal standard of humanity." Additionally, when white evangelicals do engage in race conversations, they want to control how blacks engage with them so the black person does not intimidate them or make them feel too bad. The black person must participate in the conversation in the "right way." As James Cone points out: "But even whites who acknowledge black suffering often insist that we talk about our pain with appropriate civility and restrained emotions."[59]

It is reasonable to believe the apprehension of certain people to see whiteness as the standard for what it is and to develop steps to combat its affects in our nation stems from a desire to maintain the status quo where certain people benefit from being in power or are looked at as the experts and saviors of everyone else. Cone notes:

Whites do not say much about racial justice because they are not prepared for a radical redistribution of wealth and power. No group gives up power freely. Power must be taken against the will of those who have it. Fighting white supremacy means dismantling white privilege in the society, the churches and in theology. Progressive whites do not mind talking as long as it does not cost much, as long as the structures of power remain intact.[60]

What have been some of the results of having whiteness as the preferred standard in our nation? Well, we, in effect, have two separate and unequal Americas. "In most metropolitan areas, there is still a firm division of the races between city and suburb—what a Presidential study commission once called 'two separate Americas'—that cannot be traced to any explicitly racial law."[61] But, this phenomenon, and others, can be traced to racial theology and practice. Glasser comments:

> Unemployment rates for blacks are still disproportionately and explosively higher than corresponding rates for whites, and racial stratification in employment, including public employment, is still widespread, especially in the South. Finally, blacks so frequently and disproportionately find themselves in the custody of the state, often without being convicted or even accused of any crime.[62]

Our nation has also experienced spiritual consequences from elevating whiteness at the expense of others. Financial and social outcomes may be more easily measured, but they are only one part of the conversation. "Spiritual death is another [consequence], and it is just as destructive, if not more so, for it destroys the soul of both the racists and their victims."[63]

These words violate the first commandment of any racial discussion, "Thou shalt never challenge whiteness." But, by engaging with our shared past, I hope to challenge those who accept whiteness as the standard, and force them to see that true Christian community entails equality—not just in thought—but also in deed. "As experience continues, it becomes obvious that the predominantly White society is being challenged by the attitudes and perspectives of minorities in its midst to understand that a new future life is bound to be determined by the ability of its members to enjoy a truly multiracial, pluralistic community."[64]

3

Aftereffects

"We need to know who we are in today's terms as
well as who we are historically.
Both have valid theological current."
—Clarence L. Cave[1]

Why should we care about the implications and
consequences of our culture using whiteness as the standard
for life? Because, we need to understand not only how it
has affected people and our nation in the past, but also how
it affects the thinking and attitudes of future generations,
including those who benefit, whether intentionally or
unintentionally, from whiteness, *and* those who bear the
consequences of not being white.

Systemic legacies surrounding race continue to negatively
influence future generations even though we live in a more
diverse society. "In some ways, it's super simple. People learn
to be whatever their society and culture teaches them," says
Jennifer Richeson, a Yale University social psychologist.[2]
"We often assume that it takes parents actively teaching their
kids, for them to be racist. The truth is that unless parents
actively teach kids not to be racists, they will be… It comes
from the environment, the air all around us." A study at Tufts
University found that even body language of black and white

actors interacting was enough to cause those who watched them test higher for implicit bias afterward.

"It's a myth that our country will somehow become more progressive. And it's equally a myth to think that our children will save us," Richeson says. "There's data that shows young groups like millennials are more progressive and egalitarian. But that is usually on issues like climate change or gay marriage, usually not in their level of implicit bias."

In studies of how white people react to America becoming a "majority minority" country (minorities making up over 50 percent of the population), young white subjects, including college students, were more likely to say they would rather work alongside people of their own ethnic origin.

"Yes, there have been gains in policy," Richeson says, "like allowing interracial marriage and discrimination laws, but when it comes to our interpersonal biases, it's simply not true that we just need to wait for the few old racist men left in the South to die off and then we'll be fine. The rhetoric for racism is still in place. The environment for racism is still there. Unless we change that, we cannot lessen racism."

These attitudes of whiteness as the standard can also be seen within the continuing process of "white flight," the act of whites moving away from racially diverse housing communities to less diverse areas where blacks are not wanted, or, in some cases, even *allowed* to live. White flight is a process that has been actively followed since African Americans were first allowed to purchase property and land for themselves and family members. Whites determined they didn't want "people like them." In "White America Is Quietly Self-Segregating," Alvin Chang of *Vox* reports:

> Many white people have reacted to increasing exposure to nonwhite populations, who are following in their footsteps and pursuing the traditional American dream. The reaction is not always articulated or even intentional; in fact, most people say they want to live in a diverse and integrated community; they, too, have the dream that no one will be judged by the color of their skin. But data shows

that as minorities move into suburbs, white families are making small and personal decisions that add velocity to the momentum of discrimination. They are increasingly choosing to self-segregate into racially isolated communities—"hunkering down," as [Dan] Lichter likes to call it—and preserving a specific kind of dream.[3]

One study of a group of about 200 white people showed that when they were shown several news articles on America's growing diversity, they exhibited greater bias against blacks. Washington University researcher Allison Skinner writes about the study: "These findings are consistent with a concept known as Group Threat Theory, which is the idea that when minority groups grow in size or power, the majority group feels threatened."[4] The St. Louis region, where I live, has extensive experience with white flight—white families leaving racially and economically integrated areas for locations that have less racial and economic diversity. When this occurs, much-needed resources and consistent tax revenue streams typically leave those areas as well, leaving those who remain in challenging social and economic conditions. Over the last 60 years, St. Louis has lost more than 500,000 residents.

This trend persists, and the implications are harrowing. More than half of white Americans believe the country's "way of life" needs to be protected against foreign influences, and about 84 percent of Trump supporters feel that way. Research shows many whites are now moving to "exurbs"—gated communities, unincorporated housing developments, and rural areas, explaining why the only communities with significant white growth in the U.S. are already predominantly white. "You've got one group of white Americans who are comfortable with diversity and integrating with minorities, including blacks and Hispanics and Asians," says Cornell sociologist, Dan Lichter, "and another America that is hunkering down in overwhelmingly white areas in overwhelmingly white places—and you see them moving further out."[5]

There is a certain level of irony to the researchers mentioned in Alvin Chang's article using Illinois as a place where primary research would be collected. Certain areas of Illinois bump up against the St. Louis region where there's an extensive history of racial unrest. One such instance was the East St. Louis riots of 1917, during which 3,000 white men attacked and killed between 100–200 (or more) black people and destroyed entire neighborhoods over frustrations with African American migration and the subsequent participation of blacks in the local labor force. Blacks retaliated, killing two men, which led to more attacks and destruction.

Although we have not had such extreme examples recently, the underlying tensions continue, fueling more segregation. "A lot of this is motivated by what whites do—the white reaction to minority growth, rather than what minorities themselves are doing," Lichter says. "The exposure of whites to minorities is just at a standstill, even though these communities have become more diverse. Whites are leaving these areas that are diversifying."[6]

In North Carolina, for instance, white families are using charter schools to escape the school system, and, "It's often not malicious, not overt, and not articulated. It's just the broad pattern…"[7] With whiteness as the standard, whites do not feel compelled to live any place that is too diverse for their tastes. With this pattern in full swing, it's not surprising that even religious life through our nation is still, for the most part, segregated.

A second area in which whiteness as the standard plays out in daily and political life is in the designation of whites as "the working class" over and above other groups. This designation serves as another means of allowing whites, regardless of their financial and social standing, to be compared to other groups of people and still occupy a position of superiority, even when they and the groups being compared to them are not as financially well-off. Well-to-do *and* not-so-well-to-do whites hold to the same ideas. Ta-Nehisi Coates, in an article for *The Atlantic*, says, across the economic spectrum, whites still compare themselves and their life circumstances against African Americans to feel better about themselves, as they once did in early America. The aftereffects of this, he says, are clear even today:

> The argument that America's original sin was not deep-seated white supremacy but rather the exploitation of white labor by white capitalists— "white slavery"—proved durable. Indeed, the panic of white slavery lives on in our politics today. Black workers suffer because it was and is our lot. But when white workers suffer, something in nature has gone awry. And so, an opioid epidemic among mostly white people is greeted with calls for compassion and treatment, as all epidemics should be, while a crack epidemic among mostly black people is greeted with scorn and mandatory minimums. Sympathetic oped columns and articles are devoted to the plight of working-class whites when their life expectancy plummets to levels that, for blacks, society has simply accepted as normal. White slavery is sin. Nigger slavery is natural.[8]

This elevating of the plight of white slaves over black did not occur accidentally, but by design in order to bond whites from vastly different economic statuses:

> Speaking in 1848, Senator John C. Calhoun saw slavery as the explicit foundation for a democratic union among whites, working and not: "With us the two great divisions of society are not the rich and poor, but white and black; and all the former, the poor as well as the rich, belong to the upper class, and are respected and treated as equals."
>
> On the eve of secession, Jefferson Davis, the eventual president of the Confederacy, pushed the idea further, arguing that such equality between the white working class and white oligarchs could not exist at all without black slavery: "I say that the lower race of human beings that constitute the substratum

of what is termed the slave population of the South, elevates every white man in our community."

Southern intellectuals found a shade of agreement with Northern white reformers who, while not agreeing on slavery, agreed on the nature of the most tragic victim of emerging capitalism. "I was formerly like yourself, sir, a very warm advocate of the abolition of slavery," the labor reformer George Henry Evans argued in a letter to the abolitionist Gerrit Smith. "This was before I saw that there was *white* slavery."[9]

The use of this tactic may have begun over one hundred years ago, but it is still being used today. Comments by President Nixon highlighted the honorable "nonviolence" of whites against the perceived propensity of blacks to be violent. This has long been the hallmark of politicians who believe unity is achieved by holding the "savages" down. White cultural commentators frequently carry out the trope when a group of black people gather to protest police violence.

White people are treated differently by law enforcement than blacks, especially black males. The oft-overlooked history of American policing reveals a foundation of profiling and oppressing of minorities. The St. Louis Metropolitan Police Department, of which I was a member, was initially started to protect white citizens from Native Americans as the city began to be established and expand. In fact, historically, most southern police departments began as slave patrols which traveled through areas in the South rounding up African Americans to either return them to their masters or to imprison them with the specific goal of leasing them to local corporations to perform physical labor. African Americans were leased, and worked without pay, protection, or basic human rights, while those who captured and leased them made substantial incomes from their enforced labor. The laws of the time encouraged law enforcement and the white citizenry to seize blacks on a regular basis, regardless of whether freedman or escaped slave. In 1693, court officials in Philadelphia authorized the police to "take up any Negro seen 'gadding about' without a pass or a reasonable purpose for being out."[10]

Other written and unwritten laws of the land allowed militiamen to arrest and detain a black person whose presence simply aroused suspicion. What amounted to suspicion? Being black and walking freely without being in service to a white person. The Fugitive Slave Act of 1850 threatened both law enforcement officials and ordinary citizens with severe fines if they failed to assist in the capture of a black person who was believed to be a runaway slave. Blacks had no recourse for charges brought against them, even if the charges were false, because they did not have the right to defend themselves in court. Some would argue much of this is still the case.

An officer can detain anyone who *looks* suspicious or *appears* not to belong in a location. Disagreeing or defending your right to be somewhere can lead to force, arrest, even death, with no crime committed.

How can officers use force against someone who has committed no crime? They charge you with peace disturbance and resisting arrest. What constitutes peace disturbance and resisting arrest? Not doing what you were told, even if that command was unreasonable. This is a "creative" use of the law by officers. Charge a person with an all-encompassing crime that only requires the officer to have a reasonable suspicion that something has occurred or might occur. The average citizen is then at a disadvantage because our judicial system values the testimony of officers over ordinary people.

This is only the tip of the iceberg of tactics officers use to detain and arrest people, and for the trouble that can follow a person for the remainder of their lives. Once a person is introduced to the criminal justice system, officers know it is easier to get future convictions and incarcerate people without any political or social repercussions.

There's no need to be overly dramatic about police procedures and tactics. My firsthand experience as a youth and an adult is proof enough: being harassed by police thinking I was up to no good simply because of my skin and my neighborhood. It makes little difference that I'm a seminary professor or pastor; it counts little how much good I did in communities as executive director of two nonprofits supporting the poor. I understand why none of this would be important to them, because I was one of them for five years as a police officer for the city of St. Louis.

In 2015, I wrote a book titled *Walking the Blue Line: A Police Officer Turned Community Activist Provides Solutions to the Racial Divide*, outlining my experiences serving as a police officer for the St. Louis Metropolitan Police Department. Those experiences were not very positive. As an officer, I was taught how to racially profile. I was taught that loyalty to other officers came before doing what was right. I was taught that if you didn't play the game, you could lose your life. I eventually left the department after testifying against another officer who had falsified a police report involving African American suspects.

I was taught early in my career that good policing was not about doing what was right or lawful. Good policing was about doing what was necessary to be promoted to a higher rank or transferred to a more desirable position. Generally, the two ways to be promoted or transferred are to build your arrest statistics by arresting as many people as possible in the shortest time, or to seize as much cash and drugs as possible.

This impresses supervisors. The obvious problem is that priority is given to arrests, regardless of the circumstances. Officers are tempted to make unnecessary arrests and begin to view citizens as a means to an end. Equitable application of the law becomes an afterthought.

As a young officer, I was taught that profiling was useful and necessary in conducting investigations. If a person "fits" assumptions, then they need to be investigated. A preteen male driving a brand-new Mercedes Benz should set off a red flag. Yet profiling should never be based solely on a person's skin color. Black men are easy targets, and we're conditioned to distrust and fear them. Judging by looks, we think "thug." Police do too, and most people don't care because they agree someone's appearance makes them untrustworthy. Certainly, profiling can help fight crime. But it also destroys lives.

In 2014, Michael Brown was killed in Ferguson, Missouri, near St. Louis, where I'd served as a police officer, I realized not a lot had changed since my time on the force. Not a lot has changed since Mr. Brown's death either. New stories and images of police overstepping their bounds with minorities come weekly. Before Mr. Brown, it was Eric Garner in New York being put in a chokehold that led to his death. Around the same time, a South Carolina state trooper shot an unarmed black man reaching into his vehicle to retrieve his wallet. Another South Carolina officer shot a man in the back who was running from him after a routine traffic stop. That officer was caught on video trying to plant an object at the man's body. Multiple other examples might be shared.

In 2016, St. Louis police shot an unarmed African American caregiver. The man was laying in the street with his hands in the air when he was shot. Another St. Louis officer killed a black suspect with his personal AK-47—style assault rifle, but was acquitted.

In response to the feelings of powerlessness, black communities have gone on the offensive: protesting, marching, and pushing for legislation—while others destroy, loot, and even attack officers.

In 2016, Terrence Cunningham, police chief of Wellesley, Massachusetts, offered an apology to communities of color. Chief Cunningham said the apology was necessary to "[Clear] a path that allows us to move beyond our history and identify common solutions to better protect our communities."[11] He continues:

> For our part, the first step in this process is for law enforcement…to acknowledge and apologize for the actions of the past and the role that our profession has played in society's historical mistreatment of communities of color. There have been times when law enforcement officers, because of the laws enacted by federal, state and local governments,

have been the face of oppression for far too many of our fellow citizens. In the past, the laws adopted by our society have required police officers to perform many unpalatable tasks, such as ensuring legalized discrimination or even denying the basic rights of citizenship to many of our fellow Americans.[12]

Chief Cunningham's words were met with broad support, but also dissent. Apology is a necessary first step in bridging the divide because of past practices, discrimination, and tension. His words were a welcome relief from political rhetoric offered to curry favor. It was reminiscent of other well-known words offered by leaders seeking to heal and unify people after times of turmoil. Yet not everyone wanted to hear it.

In the gospel of Luke, inspiring words from Jesus provided a vision for ancient times and for today. Recently baptized by his cousin, John the Baptist, Jesus was acknowledged to be the fulfillment of prophecies given generations before. He returned home and told anyone who would listen that he'd received a calling from God and that God had a plan to change the world. How do you think that message went over with the people who remembered him as a child?

They questioned his motives and challenged his sanity. He couldn't tell them anything. If it was St. Louis, I imagine people saying, "Boy, be quiet. You are Joseph's son. Go help him with that carpentry business he can barely keep open. Or, better yet, go give your mama some advice concerning her getting pregnant before she and Joseph were married."

Imagine if he'd come from your neighborhood. Would you believe him? Or, would you tell him to go get a real job and stop living off other people? Prophetic change agents won't be treated well during times of great social tension. In Jesus' time, there was the possibility of conflict between citizenry and the government at any time. Jewish citizens could be stopped and harassed by Roman soldiers for simply existing, and be forced to do whatever the authorities said. Jesus' ministry began when people were desperate for someone to save them from the government and social tension they were experiencing. People were actively looking for the one prophesied about, who has been promised to save them from oppression.

At the local synagogue, Jesus, the new religious teacher in town, was given the opportunity to teach, and someone handed him the scroll containing several chapters of the Book of Isaiah, arguably the most important prophetic work of the Jewish faith. Jesus read words about God's Spirit being upon him and choosing *him* to preach the message of good news to those he'd come to save—the poor, the prisoners, the oppressed, sick, and blind. The ancient prophecy was fulfilled in him, he said.

The words Jesus read aren't found in one neat section, but a compilation of two chapters within Isaiah: 58 and 61. Isaiah spoke to God's children during a time when they weren't living right. God sent Isaiah so they would turn from their wicked ways. God's primary complaint was their trusting in themselves, other people, and systems more than they trusted God.

But, they also didn't treat other people justly. One of the words used over and over in the book of Isaiah is the word *justice,* a loaded word if ever there was one. We all have a certain definition of the word. But, God's definition means treating people the way God wants them treated.

Terrell Carter's translation of Isaiah 58 would say:

> Don't get it twisted, folks. I'm less concerned about what you do in a secure religious building or at home than what you do with and for—and how you treat— your fellow man and woman. Do you help them in their times of need? Do you protect them when they're vulnerable? If I can depend on you to do these things for them, you can depend on me during your time of need, as well.

Because God's people would not trust God fully or treat other people justly, God allowed them to experience a season of military captivity. Isaiah 58 is from a time when God was trying to prepare the people for their impending freedom from captivity. Isaiah told the people they still were not where God wanted them to be spiritually or communally.

For the other section Jesus quoted, my translation would say:

> God's voice of judgment has become a voice proclaiming freedom to those held as captives. His voice speaks, anticipating that once you turn from your not-so-righteous ways and head in the right direction, God will extend freedom toward you. You no longer will be a people of sorrow and constant grief.

There is an interesting phrase here announcing the year of God's grace in Isaiah 61:1–2. In Luke 4:19, Jesus makes it current and says it's God's year to act, the Jubilee year. According to scripture, approximately every 50 years in Jewish culture—during this period of Jubilee—this was *supposed* to happen: The land was not to be worked; instead, it would rest and debts were forgiven and slaves were freed from bondage. Property gained from defaulting on a loan or a promise was returned, and the point was to give everyone a fresh start, a clean slate.

Imagine the reaction of those who heard Jesus apply these words to their time. Having experienced political, racial, and social oppression, losing their history and resources to a political force so much stronger than them, they were definitely looking forward to such a day. They sought freedom, and for God to restore them to a place of prominence within society. They were praying this restoration would occur sooner rather than later, so Jesus intended to provide his listeners with hope. Life would not remain the way it was. They all would eventually experience freedom—physical and spiritual. God would deliver them, and they would emerge from the tragedy and tears they'd shed. Their suffering would not have been in vain.

Today also, we can proclaim hope to hopeless people through racial discussions. Recognizing the pain and anguish experienced by all sides, those who have lived in tension and struggled through racial division and painful events have the opportunity to start again. We can lead the way in helping people within our nation move closer to one another, try to understand each other, and perform healing works in each other's lives. We can offer words and actions that represent the good news about forgiveness and reconciliation for those who were once enemies, but are now partners in the work of restoration. Whole communities that have experienced pain and anguish can be comforted. And, through our efforts, we can provide needed resources for greater healing, and opportunities that much of our nation has never known. We can become whole again.

Those who claim the name of Christ as Savior must make the connection between the coming of Christ to our own hurting communities, and consistently apply his universal principles to our everyday lives. When we see and treat each other as equals, when we hold the Christ's teachings about love, honor, and grace above our political principles, when we hold ourselves to the standard that we hold others, and when we live like we understand we cannot change the world on our own, then healing will begin, restoration will occur, and God's kingdom will be manifested before our eyes. This process will not be easy or fast, but it will happen and it will be worthwhile. But it will require each of us to acknowledge the parts we have played in hurting each other.

In the 1980s, characters from a greeting card line were turned into a cartoon called "The Get-Along Gang." The characters were cute, furry animal friends: Montgomery "Good News" Moose, Dotty Dog, Woolma Lamb, Zipper Cat, Portia Porcupine, and Bingo "Bet It All" Beaver. Their goal was to teach children how important it was to get along with their friends and how to work together for the betterment of others.

In the utopian world of the Get-Along Gang, life was about getting along. Life was not about making waves, but about avoiding conflict and disagreements, and getting along for the sake of getting along. In an 11-minute time frame, the cartoon characters would face a problem, each side would express their opinions, and, eventually, the character that was not getting along with everyone else would recognize the error of his/her ways and make amends.

Don't you wish life was like that cartoon? No one arguing, disagreements are minimal, and every morning you're greeted by the sun shining and theme music playing in the background. Everything solved in 11 minutes. But, in the real world, we all have opinions we want heard and we all see things in our particular ways. We have differences about almost everything, and so our relationships experience times of conflict.

The mere thought of conflict can be scary. It can immediately cause worry and nausea. I, personally, think conflict isn't necessarily bad. One of the privileges of being in relationship with one another is the fact that we don't have to agree on everything. I dare say, one of the blessings of being in relationship is the ability to have conflict, yet not let it drive us apart. Many times, conflict arises because we have a voice we want heard, and someone isn't hearing. If we're handled in a loving way, it leads to stronger relationship. Conflict can actually open doors for people to find out why they think differently and how they can move their relationships to a better place.

Of course, a main challenge is that, if not handled in a loving way, we can feel unheard and this can lead to severely damaged relationships. In conflict, we tend to think it's the other person's fault. We may come to *expect* an apology, or for them to come around to our way of thinking. We may sometimes strongly believe, as a matter of principle, it's *their* responsibility to fix the situation—and we *will not* be moved from our position.

In Matthew 18:15–20, an important question about conflict is raised: When we experience conflict, disagreement, or a separation from someone, should we wait for the other person to come and apologize to us, or should we seek to make things right with them on our own? I think Matthew 18 shows we should take the initiative in restoring the relationship. At this point in Christ's life, he's experienced multiple ministry milestones, as well as multiple instances of conflict, misunderstanding, and disagreement. The funny thing is that these conflicts, misunderstandings, and disagreements were not only with the religious leaders and Roman officials who were against him, but with his own disciples and followers.

Misunderstandings with his disciples were so frequent that we regularly read Jesus repeating the phrase, "Have I not been with you long enough for you to understand what I've been talking about, or know the meaning of what I've been teaching, or to understand my purpose?" At the beginning of Matthew 18, it seems that the disciples may have been arguing over who would be the most important person in the new kingdom, an issue they would return to in Matthew 20. This is the epitome of unnecessary conflict. Their minds were not focused on the meaning of Christ's teachings or miracles. They were thinking about who would be first in line to receive an advantageous position of authority when this great new kingdom finally came into being.

Some probably thought it would be Peter because Jesus told him he was building the new kingdom on what Peter said about Jesus being the Christ. Others may have guessed Matthew because of his political connections. Some may have hoped for one of the two sons of Zebedee, since they were some of the first disciples called. Jesus tells them they all missed the mark with their response. Instead of jockeying for position, they should have exhibited the attitude of a child. They should have had an attitude that was thankful and awestruck at God's power and love, and more aware of their own weakness and need. Jesus then told them life was hard enough already and they shouldn't make it harder for themselves or others.

He augmented his words by telling them a parable about a shepherd who left his flock of sheep to find one that wandered away (verses 10–14). It didn't matter to the shepherd how that sheep got away or why it left. What mattered was it was his responsibility to find it and bring it back to safety. Eventually, the shepherd did find the lost sheep, and he returned it to safety among the others. Jesus' point was that each person in the world holds unique value to God. Because God sees value in everyone, we should also recognize their value and treat them as God would. Even if it means we must put in some difficult and uncomfortable effort to restore them, this is the real work to be done. How many of us fully consider the implications of this before moving on to more exciting things?

During Jesus' day, people found their meaning in life from their relationships. Meaning was gained from properly fitting into an expected role, and it was lost or forfeited by stepping outside one's allotted place in society. Society was based on an honor/shame mindset. When you did what was expected of you by society and family, you brought honor to your family and self. When you did not, you brought shame to your family and yourself. Hurting or embarrassing someone was a breach of interpersonal relationships and was frowned upon by the community. It brought a dark cloud over one's social position, and even how one's family was perceived. The way to end personal and familial shame was to restore the relationship that had been broken. Forgiveness had to be granted by the hurt party for the restoration process to be complete.

Jesus adds a caveat to this process. He tells his followers to take the initiative in trying to restore a relationship, even if they were the innocent person in the situation. They were not to wait for the other person to see the light and acknowledge the error of their ways. If this act of self-initiated reconciliation did not work, they were to try it again. But, on the second time around, they were to take a few people with them. Jewish law required that when there was an accusation against someone about wrongdoing, there needed to be two to three witnesses to uphold or testify to that complaint. Ideally, this would help ensure people would not falsely accuse others. It was not to give the person someone on their side to agree with them and tell the other person to repent. It was a way to involve and preserve the larger community that would eventually be affected by the dispute. The point was not to embarrass anyone, but to restore relationships.

This kind of reconciliation is foreign to most of us. We've lost the desire to reconcile and preserve relationships with others. We prefer to remain enemies and "make others pay" for their errors from the position of adversaries, instead of remembering it's through God's love and mercy we're made sisters and brothers in God's kingdom. Life will never be perfect, and misunderstandings are bound to happen, but the current common attitude has become one of acceptance of being separated from one another. Whether in the places we live, work, or worship, we've allowed past sins to block our future relationships.

Conflict is real and unavoidable. It occurs between family members who wholeheartedly love one another, church members who truly respect and cherish each other, and people from varying ethnicities who want to have a better understanding of each other. Conflict arises because we all have our own individual faults and idiosyncrasies, and not necessarily because someone is trying to ruin our lives. Sometimes, we have conflict because we each have been raised in diverse ways with different standards. The harm is not in having the conflict or disagreement. The real damage is in how we respond to that conflict. The damage is done when we circle the wagons and point fingers and blame someone without recognizing the part we played in straining the relationship, recruit people to be on our side to prove we're right, or cross our arms against people, waiting for *them* to seek *our* forgiveness.

In the race conversation, much damage has been done. The question we all must answer is: Can we rise above our past and move forward together to cooperate in the building of God's kingdom? That kingdom will not be built through closed hearts and closed hands, or on the shoulders of the proud or those who think they are owed something. And, it will not be brought to life by people unwilling to forgive as they have been forgiven. God's kingdom will include those who have been wronged and those who have committed the wrong.

Our world, and the kingdom, needs more people who are committed to helping move the reconciliation process forward, instead of people committed to dividing and pointing fingers. Dr. Brian Peterson says, "Since the church is intended to be a foretaste of the final reconciliation of all things that God promises, Paul calls the church to start acting that way. Thus, diversity within the church is not a problem to be avoided, solved, or managed, but a gift of God's grace and a sign of the Spirit at work."[13] Dr. Holly Hearon adds:

> Reconciliation is not simply something to be desired; it becomes an imperative because we have experienced reconciliation with the one who has given us (new) life. If, in this most important of all relationships, we find that our "trespasses" (missteps) are not held against us, we too are challenged to reach across the boundaries and barriers that separate us, whether due to missteps, misunderstandings, or misconceptions, and find ways to renew our relationships...[14]

Remembering and acting as if we have been forgiven will help us forgive others, as well.

4

Finding Common Ground

"While I agree with the notion that race is an illegitimate biological concept, the ramifications of racial ideology cannot be overcome by choosing to become 'colorblind.' This position fails to recognize that on the level of lived experience, race remains part of human identity; we cannot choose to be raceless much in the same way we cannot choose to be genderless."

CHRISTOPHER CARTER[1]

For people from diverse ethnicities and backgrounds to find a mutual respect and appreciation, and work together to improve communities, sacrifice on all sides will be required. But, as we've seen, it will require more sacrifice from whites, who will have to give up the idea they can or should save others, or sometimes that their ideas of how to live and thrive are best for all. Some whites will not want to participate, although they may not admit their reasons. Some white people will only support advances for people of color when it serves their own interests.

This kind of engagement is called "interest convergence." Some whites will only agree to make changes when they can get their interests to converge with the suggested improvements. But, "if real advances are to be made in the quest for racial justice, white people must forfeit white advantage. White people, however, do not have much incentive..."[2] This also plays out in contemporary evangelical life. "White evangelicals are averse to rearranging their lives for the sake of racial justice and reconciliation. [Most of their solutions] omit financial and cultural sacrifice on the part of whites, instead maintaining 'the non-costly status quo.'"[3]

So, what are some practical solutions to the challenges surrounding race in our nation? Should we push for mass colorblindness, the belief that a person can interact with others without paying attention to their race or ethnicity? In the minds of most evangelicals, this is the solution. "Ultimately, white evangelicals simply desire to be color-blind people in a color-blind society."[4] Can seeking to be colorblind fix our race problem? Is it even possible to be colorblind? Or is it only for a privileged few? As Barbara Flagg points out, a major problem exists with this approach:

> One important form of unconscious racism is the transparency phenomenon. It is the tendency of whites not to think about whiteness, or about norms, behaviors, experiences, or perspectives that are white-specific. The transparency phenomenon makes white culture appear neutral, raceless, and normal. Transparency permits whites to disavow white supremacy while imposing white culture on people of color[5].

Besides, unfortunately, not everyone is able to disregard the color of their skin, or not have race play some part in their daily interactions. As a black man, when white people interact with me, my actions, words, and attitudes will create and reinforce unintended perceptions. Being colorblind would essentially remove the explanation for this, as well the cultural distinctions that define how I behave, believe, and interact. "In assuming that racism consists of individual attitudes and actions, color-blindness does not account for the social origins of racism. Worse yet, in seeking to remove the significance of race, color-blindness implies the elimination of the distinctive cultures of racial minorities. Color-blindness, therefore, reinforces the dominance of white culture."[6]

Walter Kim of the National Association of Evangelicals recommends we recognize race is on many people's minds, but that this does not make them racist.

> As humans, we have a finite ability to organize all the information that comes through our senses, and so of course we're going to try to come up with ways of categorizing the information. And when it comes to people, one of the ways we attempt to categorize is by the features that we see with our eyes and associate with a certain set of meanings—a person's origin or value or so-forth. This really isn't a problem just for North Americans; this is really a function of being human—the need to categorize. The real question is: Are the categories that we use appropriate, or can they be misused? And this is where we in America have gotten ourselves into a very complex and challenging situation.[7]

Multiracial Congregations

One of the first solutions for Christians in combatting racism is to make it a personal goal to spend more time with those different from us. We must become intentional about meeting and coming to know other people and their cultures. When daily life is primarily influenced by the thoughts and experiences of those like us, we're prone to assuming everyone's experiences are like ours. "Critical race theory suggests that when whites encircle whites, the transparency phenomenon takes over and white experience appears normative and normal, which can cause whites to underestimate the very real struggles of people of color within a racist social system."[8]

The suggestion to spend intentional time with others different from us goes against the comfort, logic, and advice of much of what we tend to hear. But, the need is so great in our nation, we must fight that. To change the biases, we must change our culture, starting with ourselves. Complaints about politically correct culture are common, but it's a check on what people feel comfortable expressing, and new norms of caring for others influence how we think about ourselves as well. We get messages from all around us about good and bad, and new social norms offer a check on overt racism. It's still important to challenge deep prejudice and exclusionary behavior. But to unlearn implicit biases, we need contact with others:

> It's absolutely the opposite of what white nationalists want, which is a segregated society. We need an integrated society, and at the same time need to create as much socioeconomic fairness as we can, so what relationships people have across group lines are egalitarian relationships…That is the one thing that can create trust between people on each side of an us-them divide, and the only thing in the long term I would put my money on to reduce prejudices.[9]

When was the last time you interacted with or did something with or for someone who was different than you, who had a background different from yours? If you volunteer in a food pantry, that's good. But it's safe and too controlled to provide opportunities for much interaction. Serving in those kinds of ways can be a good start, but they can also reaffirm our prejudices.

"Racial segregation of religious groups affects how we see ourselves as well as others."[10] Several biases result in our thinking, Michael Emerson says, including:

- Identifying out-group members by their differences from the in-group.
- Favoring our in-group.
- Perceiving negative behavior in out-group members as characteristic of the group.
- Recalling only information that confirms our stereotypes.

If our primary interactions with people of different races are in situations in which we only see them in one capacity, we tend to think those in their in-group are similar. If our opportunities for interaction, learning, and service only occur when we remain in positions of power and authority over others, we need to reevaluate our service. When was the last time you went somewhere where you were not the "hero" or the "expert"? When was the last time you were willing to go somewhere and become the "other," the person who did not fit in or who was the minority?

Try to form a relationship with someone you are not trying to save. Try to learn who they are and what their hopes and dreams are. Ask what their solutions are to some of our common problems and try to help implement those solutions. Stop seeing yourself as the one bringing value to a situation. Willfully becoming the other will not be convenient or easy, but you will learn more about other people and about yourself. Martin Luther King Jr. once said, "The ultimate measure of a man is not where he stands in moments of comfort and convenience, but where he stands at times of challenge and controversy."[11] In walking in the shoes of the other, you just may learn a new level of comradery and empathy.

For Christians, one way to be involved in diversity is to attend a multiracial congregation or make efforts for your church to become multiracial. One of the challenges for doing this is that many of our congregations reflect the racial division that haunts our nation. Emerson says:

> Religion in the U.S. contributes to racial division and inequality, and to cultural and political conflict, because it creates the very condition—racial segregation in an important social setting—that feeds the practices of racial categorization and the errors in perception that follow from it.
>
> Racial segregation of religious groups also affects how we interact—and with whom—by creating the ethical paradox of group loyalty. The paradox is that even if comprised of loving, unselfish individuals,

the group transmutes individual unselfishness into group selfishness.

So, in the more than 300,000 congregations in the U.S., members are busy creating group identity and forming moral persons. Those moral persons, acting morally, are aware of and help their families and the members of their own congregations first, making sure those needs are met before looking elsewhere to help. But racial segregation in congregations means we largely help people of our own race.[12]

One way to counteract this is through participation in regular worship opportunities that bridge diverse people groups. If we do not regularly engage in opportunities to learn the multiple facets of a person or people group, we will be less likely to interact with them on anything but a cursory or peripheral level. What better way to learn more about them than worshiping our common Creator together? Ryon J. Cobb, et al., argues:

Some scholars contend that participation in multiracial congregations may promote more progressive attitudes toward racial issues, particularly among Whites. Yancey, for example, reports that Whites who attend religious services with any number of Blacks exhibit a lower tendency to stereotype Black Americans when compared with Whites who attended religious services within a completely White congregation. Subsequent studies also find a positive association between attending a multiracial congregation and Whites' holding more progressive racial attitudes on issues such as interracial families and neighborhood diversity compared with Whites who attend more racially homogenous congregations.[13]

Emerson says:

Involvement in multiracial congregations, over time, leads to fundamental differences. Friendships patterns change. Through national surveys we find that people in multiracial congregations have significantly more friendships across race than do other Americans. For example, for those attending racially homogenous congregations, 83 percent said most or all of their friends were the same race as them. For those not attending any congregation, 70 percent said most or all of their friends were the same race as them. [14]

But for those attending multiracial congregations, there is a dramatic difference. Only 36 percent of people attending racially mixed congregation said most or all of their friends were the same race as them. And we found that those 36 percent were relatively recent arrivals to their racially mixed congregations.[15]

Emerson does add this caveat, "Interestingly, over 80 percent of the people in racially mixed congregations said that most of the racial diversity in their friendships came because of their involvement in their racially mixed congregation."[16]

But what does a multiracial or multicultural congregation look like? Emerson has a 20 percent rule that I think adequately defines multiracial congregations. "Research on a variety of organizations has shown that it takes 20 percent or more of another group to have their voices heard and effect cultural change on an organization. Short of that percentage, people are largely tokens. Part of this 20 percent or more rule is mathematics. At 20 percent of another group, the probability of contact across the groups is 99 percent."[17] For these reasons, Dr. Emerson defines a multiracial congregation as one having less than 80 percent of any single racial group.

A congregation may have multiple races/ethnicities, but not 80 percent of any particular people group. And, there will be multiple reasons—geography, relative affluence, and others. Extenuating circumstances may also cover a lack of effort to participate in diversity. While you cannot do anything about who lives near you, you can do several things about how you interact with the people that do live near you.

Emerson conducted extensive research and identified six core ingredients for becoming a multiracial congregation:

- *Intentionality.* Although congregations do become multiracial without intentionality, they do not stay diverse without focused intentionality. For congregations to remain diverse, they must desire to do so.
- *Diversity* as a necessary means to a larger goal. Diversity cannot be an end in itself—this is not sufficient motivation to sustain the difficulties of being diverse. Instead, diversity must be a path to a larger goal. This is often communicated in vision and mission statements.
- A *spirit of inclusion.* This can be exhibited in many ways, including through worship, small groups, diversity in who is seen providing leadership, structures that encourage cross-racial relationships, and mission statements.
- *Empowered leadership.* Leaders of multiracial congregations need to not only be diverse, be truly empowered (not tokens), and be experienced in managing diversity.
- *Adaptability.* Leaders and parishioners must develop skills of adapting to change, to each other's racial and ethnic cultures, and to each other's religious traditions and histories. Grace is essential.
- Undergirding these steps, of course, is much *faith and prayer.* Nearly all leaders of such congregations say the challenges and opportunities are too big to rely merely on themselves and their own understandings.[18]

Although I believe in diversity and am advocating intentionally working to build multiracial congregations, I also recognize this is not a painless process. There are multiple challenges. Some are easily anticipated, others are not. One of the first is that, although whites may be willing to attend diverse congregations, they may not truly believe in equality for everyone or think dissimilarly to whites not attending diverse congregations. According to some studies, white explanations for racial inequality may not be associated with whether they attend a diverse congregation or not.

A second challenge is that blacks in multiracial congregations likely already hold the same views on race as their white co-worshipers, or they adopt the racial attitudes of the whites they worship with instead of maintaining or bringing a viewpoint that is inherently different, unconsciously allowing their viewpoints on race to be modified. "Drawing on critical race theory, which views racial domination as a central organizing feature in the United States, some scholars contend that racially diverse faith communities...typically cater to the racial sensibilities of Whites."[19] So, they explain, these multiracial congregations actually end up replicating the white characteristics of the larger society.

Blacks in interracial congregations are likely to have the same thoughts about race as whites, and tend to attract other blacks who think the same way as whites in the congregation. African American attendees are actually more inclined to use "individually oriented explanations for racial inequality" than whites. "This finding would suggest that, rather than challenge dominant White racial frames that blame Blacks for inequality, multiracial congregations may (1) actually reinforce White racial frames, thus influencing minority attendees along these lines, and/or (2) attract minority attendees who are already assimilated to the dominant White culture."[20]

Blacks in such communities may be less likely to see structural inequalities, yet also less likely to see individual contributions to racism. They may be influenced "to embrace a dominant White racial frame in which the importance of structure is diminished, and such congregations could also be attractive to Blacks who already embrace those perspectives on inequality."[21]

Outside influences may also affect the racial camaraderie of any congregation. "Congregations are not immune from the racial politics echoing outside their doors... Multiracial congregations may still leave certain racial beliefs unchallenged, or even import those racial ideologies to congregants."[22] It has yet to be seen how the unity among members of multiracial congregations is being affected by politics, President Trump, and the ongoing fallout, but it will be interesting to see new data and learn how multiracial congregations coped with the external pressures of 2017 and beyond.

I still advocate for multiracial congregations because I believe they are one of the clearest examples of what eternity in God's presence will be like. We are told God's kingdom will be inhabited by multiple tribes and nations who will spend eternity worshiping together. What better way to start the choir rehearsal than together in the here and now?

Preaching about Race

Most of the suggestions here will apply to white Christians looking to contribute positively to the process of racial reconciliation. After reading this and the sources I've referred to, you may wish to know more. As James Cone wrote, "There are many whites who want to affect change but do not know when and how to do it."[23]

One of the primary tools that can be used to introduce the idea of becoming a multicultural congregation is weekly preaching. Research shows preaching can be a primary change agent, causing people to reconsider their position on any subject. Schoonmaker says, "When contemplating ethical or social issues, white evangelicals seldom accede to philosophical, scientific, or historical arguments that they cannot justify biblically… Studies suggest that preachers can change evangelical minds about race by stirring evangelical hearts about race."[24]

For those who take up the challenge to preach about race, there are a few things to consider. First, preaching about race cannot be occasional, once or twice a year. For any meaningful change in attitudes, preaching about race must occur on a regular basis until the idea has fully taken root. To accomplish this, a preacher must develop a long-term plan for teaching and preaching prophetically about race. A person should take the time to make an intentional plan to address the subject on at least a quarterly basis. This can be accomplished through utilizing the lectionary and looking for opportunities to talk about race that naturally arise from scripture.

For example, passages from Jonah, scriptures concerning the reasons why Old Testament Israel was in regular warfare with other nations, passages about relationships between different nations, or the story of Peter's vision about the white sheet filled with animals and his subsequent conversations with Cornelius and church leaders can all be used as springboards to begin the conversation with your congregation. Also, holidays or cultural events such as Martin Luther King Day, Black History Month, Women's History Month, etc., are great opportunities to introduce the conversation.

Creativity is necessary when developing a sermon or preaching series about race so people can interact with the ideas in encouraging ways, rather than depressing. In one church I served, we used Broadway musicals to introduce ideas about race, class, and disabilities—*Les Miserables, Huck Finn, The Hunchback of Notre Dame,* and *Fiddler on the Roof.* For the sermon involving *Huck Finn,* two high school seniors performed the major roles, and I co-preached with our white pastor. The contrasts between the actors and preachers highlighted the points of the sermon.

A second challenge is to preach prophetically. Reminding people how their past has influenced their present while providing hope for their future, Rev. Dr. C. Anthony Hunt says:

> [I]t was generally the task of biblical prophets to speak to real conditions and concerns, which existed among Hebrew people—and to call people back into covenant relationship with God (and others). The biblical prophets, thus, stood with one foot in the past—reminding Israel of its history in God—and with one foot in the future, helping them see where God wanted them to go.[25]

Using Hunt's assessment, a prophetic sermon would:

- Address the past – *What has happened to cause us to end up where we are?*
  - Ask/identify the foundational practices/beliefs in your context that reinforce separation and segregation.
  - Ask: Is God, history, or local tradition being used as the excuse to keep things a certain way / keep certain people out?
  - Do not talk about theory. Give concrete examples/experiences that listeners will recognize or be able to identify with.
- Recognize where you currently are – *Where are we now?*
  - Be truthful about current standing.
  - Do it in love, in a way that does not attack anyone or point fingers.
  - Ask if this is the best that God has for you.
- Provide hope for the future–*Where can we go in the future with God's help?*
  - Remind what God wants for our human relationships.
  - Remind what God says about the future of human relationships.
  - Hold Christ up as the example of reconciliation.
- Encourage heading in the direction God wants for all.
  - Show movement from hearing to *acting* through practical ideas for participation.
  - Through a cross-cultural event, whether at your location or in a different community, challenge people to go and get involved.
  - Provide/suggest opportunities for people to build a relationship with the "wrong" type of person (maybe adopt a school in a different neighborhood).
  - Encourage people to become students of other races/communities instead of being observers with opinions.

If you decide to intentionally preach about race to help build a multiracial congregation, be aware of the challenges.

You will likely experience pushback from the congregation. This doesn't mean they are bad people or necessarily against racial equality. It is simply hard to talk about race. It's uncomfortable to face the limits of our experience with other races, with racism, and our responses to them. Guilt over our actions, beliefs, and our family histories complicate people's thinking about their responsibility to them. Some simply will not want to acknowledge their prejudice. It will be up to you to discern the difference.

Another area of concern is whether to use theological language. Much historical theological language involves "light vs. dark," with white as God winning every time. Common theological language also holds up "slavery" as a positive disposition for Christians to follow. While it's valid to express our commitment to Christ, it can suggest very uncomfortable triggers for some. As one writer said, "[I]t is a lot easier to call yourself a slave for Christ when there is no memory of slavery in your family."[26] Develop good relationships with people of differing races and let those relationships serve as sounding boards for you in better understanding what words and concepts faithfully express the common humanity and value we all share before God.

Other Ideas to Consider

In addition to preaching, other options exist for helping move a congregation toward racial reconciliation. Consider developing and articulating a "theology of racial reconciliation" with and for church leadership, to include in your congregation's core documents—vision statement, mission statement, etc. For example, these are from two well-known congregations:

River City Community Church in Chicago–"*We are on a quest to become a multi-ethnic community of Jesus followers that transform the city of Chicago through worship, reconciliation, and neighborhood development.*"[27]

Riverside Church in New York–"*Our mission is to serve God through word and witness; to treat all human beings as sisters and brothers; and to foster responsible stewardship of God's creation."*[28]

These short, concise statements convey a clear intention for the congregations.

Another idea: Open certain practices or areas of church life typically reserved for church members to nonmembers. Allow nonmembers to sing in the choir or lead special music from their cultural heritage. Invite participation in leading certain portions of the worship service, such as reading scripture or serving as ushers. Extend grace to nonmembers to serve on nonfinancial and nonlegal committees. Open the church to leading "English as a Second Language" courses or G.E.D. courses to let people know your congregation is welcoming to people serving in ways that are meaningful to them.

Also identify a congregation different from yours and begin conversations about developing a regular relationship by "adopting" that church. You might agree to fellowship a specific number of times together each year, or commit to assisting them with a certain number of mission projects each year, and/or exchanging pulpits a certain number of times a year. The goal would be for each church to commit to multiple opportunities of service together. Additionally, you could consult with multiple pastors of local congregations and join or start a "federation" of churches in your community to meet on a regular basis for fellowship and to address a community need. You could also join a peer learning group, reading and discussing books that deal with race. In building relationships across racial lines in these ways, you will normalize interactions with people you may not regularly spend time with.

Your congregation could also consider adopting an organization that serves people different from those who currently make up the majority of your congregation. If your congregation is historically white, you could adopt a school that primarily serves minority students. You could provide tutoring, mentoring, or coaching to children from the school. Or, you could adopt a business that serves a population different from your own. You can find companies that are primarily minority- or women-owned by contacting your local small business administration office or by contacting small business incubators that specialize in serving minority and immigrant populations.

Your congregation could seek to partner with a local police or fire department, or emergency medical provider and allow them to use your building as space for monthly community meetings. This provides community members with an opportunity to engage in conversation with these groups within neutral spaces. You could also explore ways to volunteer with local law enforcement agencies. For example, you could become a "Citizen on Patrol" representative or a chaplain. By working closely with departments like this, you will gain valuable exposure to multiple people groups on a regular basis.

The strongest recommendation I have for anyone who wants to see racial equality play out in real life is to stop being silent when you see, hear, or read racially divisive things. I agree with Cone when he says, "I urge white theologians, ministers, and other morally concerned persons to break their silence immediately and continuously."[29] I know that immediate and continual participation from people who may not have a clear idea of how they fully feel about the conversation is a tall order, but I believe all of us are up for the task. "Talking about how to destroy white supremacy is a daily task and not just for consultations and conferences. If we only talk about white supremacy at special occasions set aside for that particular issue, the problem will never be solved."[30]

We may tire of having racial issues brought up, but we cannot tire of participating. The process is underway of fixing our nation's extensive history of failure relating to race. Whites must remember they're not the only ones dealing with this—just the most recent. "Bigotry and hatred are not the most urgent problems. The most urgent, the most disgraceful, the most shameful and most tragic problem is silence. Theologians and ministers, churches, synagogues and associations must not remain onlookers—that is, silent in the face of hate, in the face of brutality, and in the face of mass murder."[31]

Instead of addressing the historic effects of racist practices and policies, some would rather point out the sins of blacks and how they need to clean up their own communities before they hold whites accountable for their perceived sins. Cone provides an adequate response: "That the oppressed are sinners too is a very important point to make but often hard to hear, especially when it is made by the oppressor. The ever-present violence in poor communities is at least partly due to the sins of the oppressed. We must never assume that God is on the side of the oppressed because they are sinless but rather because of God's solidarity with weakness and hurt—the inability of poor people to defend themselves against violent oppressors."[32] It is understandable why some whites would miss this, but it's important to recognize and speak out against the sins of their own community first.

This change from silence to vocal support of African Americans cannot only occur on a local level. It must also occur on the larger denominational and educational levels. "To create an antiracist theology, White theologians must engage the histories, cultures and theologies of people of color. It is not enough to condemn racism. The voices of people of color must be found in your theology. You do not have to agree with their perspectives but you do have to understand them and incorporate their meanings in your theological discourse."[33]

Who Is Your Enemy?

Who is your enemy? Who do you just not like? What person or group do you despise? Maybe it's Donald Trump and other Republicans. Through their efforts to repeal the Affordable Care Act, attempts to fund a wall to divide southern portions of our nation from Mexico, and calls to deport anyone they think doesn't deserve to live in America, they've done enough lately to make certain populations in America angry. Or, maybe it's the Democrats you can't stand.

They don't seem to understand the value of challenging work or earning your way in the world. They would rather put someone on a government program and give them a handout instead of teaching them how to make a way for themselves.

Or, maybe it's the people who support Black Lives Matter, and don't respect police officers. Maybe you think they act like terrorists and animals and should be treated as such. Or, maybe it's the police, who seem not to care about people of certain races, and abuse their power. Or, maybe it's the media, the purveyors of "fake news," those who exist to keep our nation divided about anything and everything. Or perhaps it's a co-worker who jumps at every opportunity to take credit for work they did not do. Maybe it's a neighbor who won't keep their dog from squatting in your yard.

What would it take for you to experience peace within that relationship? Would it require an apology? Would it take them going somewhere else and leaving you alone? What would it take?

We are not the first people to have to think about who we're separated from and what we would require from someone else to fix the relationship. There are multiple examples from Jesus' life, but there's another as well.

Jonah's Judgment

At its core, the book of Jonah is about how Jonah responds when he finds out God cares about the people Jonah cannot stand. The book is about the challenge Jonah faces as God asks him to change his thinking toward people he's hated for many years—with good reason. The challenge he faced, and initially failed at, was even attempting to see these people as God saw them. Jonah's struggles parallel our own as they relate to the discussion of race and racial reconciliation.

Jonah came from a town called Gath-hepher and was the son of Amittai. He was a prophet active during the eighth century b.c.e. The only other time he's mentioned in the Hebrew Bible is in 2 Kings 14:23–27, where reference is made to a prophecy he'd given of a certain land being returned to God's children. Not much else is known about him. What we do know is that, one day, Jonah is minding his own business and God gives him a task to complete. He was to go to Nineveh and tell the people of that city to change their ways or experience God's wrath.

This is a simple and straightforward command from God, but Jonah refused. He hated Nineveh and everything it stood for. Located to the west of Jonah's town, it was a city about three miles wide and the largest in the area at the time. It was tremendously pagan and its inhabitants were known for participating in witchcraft and sorcery. More importantly, it was the capital of the Assyrian Empire. The Assyrians were one of the primary enemies of Israel, Jonah's people. And, the Assyrians were growing in power and reputation. They regularly threatened Israel with violence as they expanded their dominance over the area. All God's children knew Assyria was working toward conquering them and taking their land.

And, then God does the unimaginable and tells Jonah to go to them and preach repentance so God could save them. How would you respond if God told you to go to your enemies and preach repentance to them? We might wonder why God would ask something so goofy in the first place. *God, they don't even believe in you. They have their own gods. They don't like my people. They will either imprison me or kill me as soon as they find out I'm from Israel. I don't want them to repent. I want to see them dead for everything they've done to my people and our land. I want to see them suffer, not let off the hook.*

Jonah had multiple reasons, so he refuses and hops on a boat going in the opposite direction. A terrible storm occurs and the crew panics and begins to call out to every god in the book in hopes that one of them will cause the storm to stop. Eventually, Jonah confesses he's the source of their troubles and urges them to toss him overboard. When they do, the storm stops and a great fish swallows him.

Jonah made multiple mistakes. First, he allowed his prejudices to stop him from being obedient to God's instructions. God created the people of Nineveh and loved them as passionately as Israel and Judah. Jonah allowed his anger to cloud his judgment. When we do not love others, we put ourselves outside of the will of God.

Second, Jonah's personal prejudice caused him to prioritize his feelings above the salvation of an entire city. His anger caused him to take the fate of an entire people into his own hands. He decided that he, not God, was the best person to decide their fate—and his personal judgment against them was death. They deserved it, for justice. However, he was not God and neither do we have the right to determine what's just for someone else, especially when God has told us what to do for them to help them experience life in relationship with others.

Third, Jonah's personal prejudices against Nineveh caused him to jeopardize the lives of innocent people, especially the people on the boat traveling to Tarshish. These people were living their lives as normal. They likely hadn't done anything wrong that day outside of giving Jonah a ride. Some would argue they were not necessarily innocent because they likely weren't of Israel or Judah and didn't know who God was. But, does that make them evil people? They were likely just like you and me, trying to make an honest wage. Then their lives were threatened because Jonah was mad at someone else.

Finally, Jonah's personal prejudices against Nineveh caused him to endanger his own life. When he decided to ignore God's directive for him, he took his fate into his own hands. The problem with that is obvious. Jonah was no competition to God. God would be obeyed, whether Jonah wanted to or not. And, unfortunately, Jonah would experience pain and turmoil for doing what he wanted instead. Whenever we do that, we will inevitably put ourselves in precarious predicaments.

The foundation of the book of Jonah is the fact that God loves all created beings and wants to be in relationship with them—even when *we* do not get along with them or like them. God pursues us out of love. And, every now and then, God calls us to participate in this process, even when we consider those people our enemies. Rev. Joel Schreurs says:

Few of us (hopefully, none of us!) have an actual list of enemies in our desk drawers. But that doesn't mean that we do not have a file tucked away in our minds of the people we have labeled "enemies." Some of these people have hurt us. Others have simply annoyed us. There is the neighbor whose dogs howl late into the night. The co-worker who manages to take credit for every good thing we do. The guy at school who knows how to magnify every already embarrassing moment. These "enemies" may not have committed atrocities on the scale of the Assyrians. But that doesn't mean that we are any more eager to extend to them the love, mercy, and compassion of Jesus.[34]

Rev. Schreurs goes on to say:

Scholars often present Jonah as a representative of the people of Israel—a sort of microcosm of his nation and, more specifically, his nation's failures. According to this line of thinking, God called both Jonah and Israel to be a blessing to the nations. Both Jonah and Israel, however, resisted this call. Instead of seeing themselves as conduits for God's blessing, they began to clutch God's blessings to their chests and refused to share with the nations around them. They became myopic and self-centered, insisting that YHWH was their God and was (or at least should be) interested only in being their god—and not the god of their neighbors.[35]

Jonah shows this type of attitude throughout the book. In chapters three and four, his negative attitude toward Nineveh turns into righteous indignation with God. In chapter two, Jonah called out to God from the belly of the fish and pleaded for God's mercy and forgiveness, promising that if he ever gained his freedom from the beast, he would obey and go to Nineveh. God answered his prayer. In chapter three, Jonah was spit out by the great fish, but he didn't get much time to celebrate because God delivered to him the same message that sent him running in the first place. "Go to Nineveh." This time, Jonah immediately obeyed. He traveled to the city and told them to repent.

The people were fearful and believed him. They decided to fast and wear sackcloth as a means of showing God they believed and were willing to do what God wanted. More people heard Jonah's words, believed, and followed suit. This process of hearing the message, believing it, and deciding to fast and repent continued until word reached the king of the city. He too believed the message and was so convinced that he left the royal palace in fear and sat in dust as a sign of his willingness. His royal court also followed his example. He eventually commands everyone in the city to get in line and repent. And this was to apply not just to the people, but even to their livestock. Even their cows and horses would have to fast along with their masters.

This is the dream of any pastor or evangelist, isn't it? To preach a sermon and 100 percent of those who hear it believe it and start to live accordingly. They tell others and start to live as you told them to. Eventually, the president hears and believes and makes everyone act accordingly. Every preacher I know would be doing cartwheels. However, Jonah isn't happy. As one preacher has said, "[Some translations] play down his anger with the words 'this was very displeasing to Jonah and he became angry.' The Hebrew reads roughly, 'it was evil to Jonah, a great evil, and his anger burned.' Sounds like righteous indignation to me."[36]

But, why is Jonah angry and who is his anger for? Well, he's angry that God would be willing to forgive these people. "Jonah is angry at God for the very attributes that Israel has always depended on for its own salvation!"[37]

"The short answer is because God loves too many people."[38] Another way of saying it is that God tends to love the "wrong" people (in some people's minds—including Jonah's). Jonah's mind is stuck on the idea that maybe, just maybe, God will let his enemies die. And, if not, maybe their city will at least be ransacked or hit with a tremendous natural disaster. But, that was not God's plan. God wanted to bring this group of people into relationship with the Holy. Jonah could not get his mind around it. God was *his nation's* God, and not anyone else's. This sounds like the political rhetoric, America is our nation and should be kept for Americans. Frances Flannery writes, "...Jonah did not want to extend his circle of compassion outside of his comfort zone, while God's care encompassed every creature."[39]

This is not only a problem for Jonah and the people of Israel. It's a problem we face, even in the twenty-first century. We live in a country in which too many say: if you're not on our side, if you don't believe exactly like we believe, if you're not willing to give your loyalty to causes we deem most important, you are not only our enemy, but we hope something goes wrong in your life. Obviously, this is the wrong viewpoint. John Holbert offers this:

> The tale tells us who the bum is. He is any religious person who claims to know God, and to follow the ways of God. This person can quote the scripture, as Jonah does several times, can pray up a storm, or in Jonah's case after a storm in a fish's belly, can imagine herself as a prophet of God. But in reality, this person is the rankest of hypocrites. Scripture serves only their purposes, and God is their lap dog, called upon to affirm the narrow things they already believe. In short, Jonah is a prophet gone bad, a religious mountebank, an ecclesiastical huckster. Unfortunately, Jonah did not die a long time ago; he is alive and well and living among us, and too often, in us.[40]
>
> "Whenever we read the Bible and use it to exclude, deny, and reject living creatures of God, there is Jonah. Whenever we say we will follow God—"Here am I, send me," we sing—but in fact follow our own bigoted desires, our own narrow-minded ways, there is Jonah. Whenever we hope that persons who are not like us, who do not sound like us or think like us or act like us, should be removed from the earth by some edict of God, there is Jonah. Jonah, like the Frankenstein monster, keeps getting

reborn to wreak havoc on the world that God has loved and redeemed.[41]

Talking about this can make us seem cranky. Yet we all need to see race and the discussions we have around the subject in a way that honors our differences and the God who created us all. God calls us to view all people as equal and treat them appropriately. Our claims to being God's children are not verified by the fact that we attend church every Sunday or volunteer our time for multiple worthy causes, but by how we love others, especially those who are different from us.

Conclusion

"We need to challenge the norm in our culture that places the responsibility of diversity, including appropriate use of language, on minorities themselves. If we are striving to move toward a more inclusive society, indeed a more inclusive Christianity that values all of God's creation, then this responsibility needs to be shared by all and prioritized by those in positions of power and influence in order to ensure enduring change."
—CHRISTOPHER CARTER[1]

You remember what the best way to eat an elephant is, of course—*one bite at a time.* Most of us have heard that before. But, how many of us know where it comes from? Former U.S. Army General Creighton W. Abrams fought in multiple wars, including WWII, eventually leading U.S. forces in Vietnam and becoming Chief of Staff for the Army. General Abrams was asked how he, as the leader of many troops, could keep his life and job in perspective when things did not look as if they were going to go the way he planned. How was he able to keep things in perspective and stay motivated when a challenge looked insurmountable? He responded that it would be easier to eat an elephant if a person does it one bite at a time.

It's an encouraging idea for many people. Multiple songs, books, and articles have used the phrase. It's influential because it summarizes wisdom that's been shared throughout the ages. It is a timeless truth that the best way to solve any problem is to break it down into smaller, more manageable pieces. If you try to tackle a problem all at once without fully understanding its pieces, you probably will not fully understand the problem and therefore won't be able to solve it. When you can figure out the smaller, more manageable pieces, you can figure out how to solve the whole problem.

General Abrams is just one in a lengthy line of influential people who have shared this type of advice. A quote often misattributed to Winston Churchill or Abraham Lincoln is: "Success is the ability to go from one failure to another with no loss of enthusiasm." Irish author Samuel Beckett said, "Ever tried. Ever failed. No matter. Try again. Fail Again. Fail better." I like this idea of taking multiple steps to solve a problem or to figure something out. I can give multiple examples from my personal life when I was faced with an elephant of a problem and the only way to make my way through it was to take small steps. It's like the old saying, "The journey of 1,000 miles begins with one step." I imagine most of us have followed this type of advice throughout our lives.

As much as I agree with General Abrams, is there ever a time when we should be doing something different? Is there ever a time when we should look at a challenge, or a problem, or an opportunity and jump in head first? Can you think of an example of when taking the time to better understand a challenge ultimately backfired? I am reminded of the old saying, "Sometimes we cannot see the forest for the trees." Sometimes, when focusing on the details, we risk not seeing the big picture. We miss the overall beauty or significance of something. Life is a balancing act between seeing the forest and the trees. Sometimes our focus needs to be on the forest, sometimes it must be on the individual trees. The challenge we all face is how to enjoy the beauty of the forest without missing the beauty of each individual tree that forms it.

Balancing the bigger picture against the smaller details is very important to the ideas in this book. The challenges we face in understanding each other while acknowledging past actions that have adversely affected others, while trying to live in community with others, are serious and significant. We have the privilege of living with and among imperfect people who have different opinions and varying degrees of belief about things.

When it comes to the subject of race and racial reconciliation, there are always going to be multiple sides to be considered. We will not all see things the same way, regardless of whether we're all Christians or not. People who belong to the same faith, read the same Bible, and regularly participate in worship together may have vastly different responses and opinions on the subject—and those varying opinions will come from people who claim the same faith foundation.

There is a clear struggle in the community of faith about who we think can and cannot be included. In some ways, it sometimes seems like the Church with a big "C" is more divided than unified—and one of the most disheartening things about this is that the entire world is watching. And, sometimes, it's hard for them to be able to distinguish the attitudes of the Church from those of the world.

It is never an easy task, whether in the world or in the church, to talk about the things we disagree on, including racism and reconciliation. That usually entails someone acknowledging that some type of wrong was committed and apologizing for it. The good thing is that we're not the first to have to deal with what it means to live in community with people as different from us as night and day. Paul's letter to Titus was written to a person leading a diverse group of people trying to understand what it meant to be equal members of Christ's body and grow in faith and their commitment to God and one another.

Paul tells Titus that one of the reasons he's writing is the ever present potential for diverse opinions leading to division. Toward the end of the letter, Paul challenges Titus to take a stand. He tells Titus to share the principles he's given him, as the basis for relationship with God and others. "Practice love and grace in your own life and teach other people to do the same thing," he basically says. Teach them to love one another—whether in their marriages, with their children, or with neighbors and friends.

Their lives should reflect a love that comes when they understand God's love and grace has been given to them through Jesus the Christ, and their privilege is to show that same love and grace to other people. Teach the people to never forget where it is they've come from, he says. Remind them they are no better than anyone else, that what they have in life comes from God because God has forgiven them, just like God is willing and able to forgive anyone else through the sacrifice of Christ. The principles of love and grace are the essentials relationship with God and one another is based on.

Although I didn't write this book to win a specific argument, I hoped to respectfully acknowledge there are varying opinions about race and how it has affected people and our nation's development. Just because people have different opinions about race and its place in society does not make them less acceptable to God or automatically an enemy.

I agree with Paul's advice to Titus to tell people the truth about God and God's desires for how people should treat each other. If a person listens and abides by that truth, good. If they do not, they will eventually have to answer for their actions and attitudes. Paul tells Titus not to waste time on those kinds of people, but instead concentrate on supporting others of the faith who listen and try to abide by the truth. Titus is to continue to teach those kinds of people how to live and remind them God is pleased with them.

This book has been an attempt to follow Paul's practical advice to make a difference in people's lives. David Anderson said, "Paul is interested in how the knowledge of the truth affects our day to day lives. Remember, the apostle is a practical man... He isn't just interested in theory, he is interested in godliness, and he knows that a right knowledge of the truth leads to godliness."[2] If this book helps a handful of people change their views about people different from them, I will have contributed to the process of helping a few people become godlier.

Obviously, one book can't answer every question or concern about the subject of race. Race is a complex issue with many nuances. In some ways, this book only begins to scratch the surface. I admit the solutions I've provided are simple because we have a challenging time implementing even the simplest changes, let alone deeply complex practices. Attempting to follow the simple suggestions in prior chapters will require intentional buy-in and sacrifice from all of us.

This is a journey we all take together. Sometimes we will need to move quickly to implement changes on personal and corporate levels. At times, it may seem we're flying by the seats of our pants. On other occasions, we'll need to move slowly and deliberately to make sure voices are given equal time and respect. No matter how we move, we must remember why we're moving in the first place. We engage in conversations because we want all people treated as though they truly reflect God's image—because they do.

Someone once said, "When languishing for solutions, don't ask, 'Have I got the correct answer?' What you should ask is, 'Have I got the correct question?'" The correct question for readers is, "Do we view those different from us as equal in value to God?" This may require some of us to learn to think and communicate in innovative ways. But, more than that, it will require a change of heart evidenced by the ways we treat other people. This process will not be easy, but it can happen. Francis of Assisi once said that when you're trying to do something it seems will never be accomplished, the first step is to "start by doing what's necessary; then do what's possible; and suddenly you are doing the impossible."[3]

Conflict Management

However, we cannot forget that although we may earnestly try to live in loving community with others, this does not mean it's possible to live in conflict-free community. As long as there are people in the world, there will be a certain level of tension present. It seems conflict is one thing guaranteed to occur in all families—even Christian families. Have you ever been involved in a family fight? When we were kids, I fought with my twin brother Derrell on a regular basis. When we fought, it was usually because I was being a bully and picking on him.

I remember one night when Derrell was sleeping and I decided it would be fun to scare him awake by taking two baseball bats and knocking them together over his head. I banged the bats together and, as I hoped, it did scare him awake. However, he also sat up in bed, startled, and bumped his head into the two bats. He was not happy about this Louisville Slugger alarm system and a fight ensued. Another time, we fought because it was the NBA playoffs and I was rooting for the Lakers because they had purple and gold jerseys and Derrell was rooting for the Celtics because they had green jerseys. The Lakers were winning and I was rubbing it in Derrell's face. A shoving match ensued and our grandfather had to intervene.

When we fought, it never was about anything important. It was always about something petty or goofy. It didn't make sense for us to fight over any of it. It never failed that when we got into a fight, Grandma or Papa would break it up and punish us. It didn't matter who started it; we both were punished. Grandma's favorite punishment was to make us sit in chairs with our backs to each other. We could not get up from our seats or talk to each other. We couldn't do anything but sit in the kitchen and listen to each other breathe. Grandma would make us sit like this for a good period of time and, at some point, we would start arguing.

But, before letting us go our separate ways, Grandma would tell us how unfortunate it was for us to fight each other. She would ask a series of questions: Why were we fighting? Why would we want to hurt someone we loved who was our flesh and blood? Why would we want to hurt someone we looked just like? She told us we should spend time protecting each other instead of fighting, because, when worse came to worse, all we really had in life was each other. I'm happy to say that as we got older, Derrell and I stopped fighting and began to appreciate each other. We learned to love each other the way brothers should. We eventually became each other's biggest protectors and advocates.

In dealing with the challenges facing the Church today, we can acknowledge that we won't always get along or agree on everything. Derrell and I were not the first brothers to have an argument. Disagreements and tension are part of the life cycle of every human relationship and every church. We are reminded of this in Paul's letter to the church at Galatia. The letter is filled with examples of tension and disagreement between multiple people. In Galatians 2:11–21, we see the aftereffects of an argument between Paul and Peter.

The tension Paul and Peter experienced came from the fact that the early church leaders were working through whether non-Jewish people could be equal to Jewish people if they didn't follow the long-held traditions the Jewish believers followed. Tension was present because Paul believed if God said everyone gained sufficient and equal salvation through the blood and sacrifice of Christ, then following rituals and traditions could not be a requisite for inclusion in God's family. For Paul, the local church and the universal Church must include all people in the body of Christ, in the commonly held grace found in Christ.

Those requiring non-Jewish persons to participate in circumcision were trying to take away the freedoms everyone had in Jesus, the Christ. The fact that these leaders were witnessing God doing some dramatic things through non-Jewish people, even without them being circumcised, was not good enough for them. They wanted everyone to participate in certain rituals. Eventually, the leaders of the church came to an agreement about non-Jewish believers remaining uncircumcised and Paul continuing to evangelize within their communities.

And, life was good. So good that Peter eventually came to where Paul was and began to treat non-Jewish people like good friends. Peter even spent time in their homes and ate with them. But, things did not stay good for long. People from Jerusalem eventually came to where Paul and Peter were and Peter changed his attitude and actions toward non-Jewish people because he did not want to be accused of being too friendly. Paul was not happy with Peter and called him two-faced.

Apparently, Peter was not alone. Multiple people turned their backs on Paul and his non-Jewish friends so they wouldn't look bad in front of people who saw the law as equal to God's grace. Dr. Gregory H. Ledbetter says:

> While there were no explicit prohibitions against eating with Gentiles, observant Jews sought increasingly to eliminate any contact with non-Jews for the sake of the purity of their faith. Antioch, the place of Paul and Peter's confrontation, was a veritable mixing pot of people, cultures, and faiths. The tumbling of the old dividing walls of all kinds made utter sense to Paul, under the new freedom of Christ, but created a crisis for isolationist Jews and, as a result, Jewish Christians.[4]

The argument that Paul was having with Peter, and the other leaders of the church, was bigger and more important than anything Derrell and I used to argue about. It was about the new freedom available through Christ: Freedom to love and interact with anyone, just as they were. Dr. Alicia Vargas says, "The great theme of Paul's letter to the Galatians is Christian freedom."[5] Unfortunately, Peter was willing to believe in this freedom as long as no one from Jerusalem or the conservative group of believers was watching.

Peter was missing out on the freedom available through faith. Dr. Alan Brehm says, "Basically, the point of much of what Paul was trying to do in his ministry was to help people find freedom from everything that could make them feel trapped."[6] Paul did not want people to feel trapped by the law or tradition or other people's unrealistic agenda-driven expectations. Paul was going to fight against those things. Paul realized and tried to share with other people that Christ's death and resurrection was not only to reconcile and unite people to God, but also to reconcile and unite people to each other, whether or not they came from the same cultural background.

Paul was not foolish enough to think this kind of reconciliation would be a painless process. As one who had previously built his lifestyle upon following the law, he knew it would take time for people to understand what freedom in Christ looked like. But, though he knew this, that didn't mean he was okay with what Peter was doing. Paul understood the value of Peter agreeing with him and living out this reconciliation among non-Jewish people. Peter's approval could influence so many more people and help to change many minds. But, Peter did not stick to his new understanding of God's grace. That's one reason Paul was so frustrated.

Throughout Galatians, Paul speaks to the difficulty of sorting out what Christianity would be as it moved from its base among Jesus' Jewish followers into a world of non-Jewish people. In a sense, one of the challenges we all face is dealing with the following questions: What will our world look like if we invite those who are different from us to regularly participate in life with us? What will our churches look and sound like if people from multiple ethnicities and historical experiences join together? Will our communities still be recognizable? Will our treasured songs sound the same? Will we become marginalized and powerless or lose our influence?

I understand and respect the hesitation that Peter and the Jerusalem disciples were experiencing. Things were changing around them so quickly. Things they thought were supposed to be one way were changing and becoming something else. But, the change was God-ordained. And, that change eventually benefitted the entire world. In many ways, we are like Peter and the other disciples. We appreciate the familiar. We appreciate when life is steady and predictable. We appreciate being in relationship with people just like us. But, we cannot forget that one of the reasons Christ died for us was to give us certain freedoms. Freedom to be in relationship with each other in all the diversity that we share.

Mandela's Example

Nelson Mandela was President of South Africa from 1994–1999. President Mandela's life was too grand and impactful to fully describe here, but, during much of his life, South Africa was governed under the rules of apartheid, the Jim Crow of South Africa, dividing it along racial lines so that whites enjoyed great benefits while blacks had few rights.

Mandela was a leader in grassroots efforts to try to change South Africa's stringent racial laws. Because of his stance against racial segregation, he was eventually arrested for treason against the state, tried in court, and sentenced to life in prison. While Mandela was imprisoned, he experienced physical and psychological abuse from the prison guards who were charged with his care. He experienced years of mental and physical pain. The guards who subjected Mandela to abuse did it because they were in power over him and could never imagine a day when Mandela would be out of prison, once again living as a free man.

They also could not imagine a day when Mandela would be elected president of their country. If they could have, they probably would not have treated him as they did. But, as fate would have it, Mandela was eventually released from prison, and subsequently elected. On that momentous day, I can imagine those prison guards asking, "Will Mandela come after us, seeking revenge?"

When was the last time you had to ask for forgiveness from someone for something you did? Saying you were wrong and asking forgiveness may be a process you're not used to. I had one relative growing up who said, "I may not always be right, but I'm never wrong." Essentially, he was saying he knew he made mistakes in life, but he didn't feel he should have to apologize for them.

Asking or seeking forgiveness from someone else is not a pleasant thing. It is emotionally and psychologically uncomfortable. It involves admitting something is wrong and that you played a part in making it that way. Seeking forgiveness from someone else puts you in a place of vulnerability, as well. If you must go to someone and ask them for forgiveness, you run the risk of embarrassing yourself, because that person may decide they don't want to forgive you. You also may be concerned that if you apologize or ask someone to forgive you, it will make you look weak. Your bigger concern may be about saving face.

Let me ask a different question. When was the last time you were asked to accept forgiveness from someone else? When was the last time you were the one approached for forgiveness? How did that make you feel? What was your response?

Those prison guards never went to Mandela and sought his forgiveness. Instead, Mandela was the one who initiated the process of healing. He contacted them and invited them to meet with him so they could talk and move on with their lives. Mandela had already forgiven the guards for what they'd done to him. They didn't have to ask forgiveness and they would not have to fear what he might do to them.

Mandela's act of forgiveness was even bigger than an initial conversation with them. He eventually invited those guards that had formerly abused him in prison, as well as the officials who conspired to have him imprisoned, to his inauguration dinner as president and gave them prominent seating at the event. He did not embarrass them or use them as an object lesson about the negative things he experienced. Over the years, Mandela talked about the process he had to go through mentally and emotionally to be able to forgive them. He acknowledged that none of it had been easy, and it did not occur quickly. His ability to forgive occurred over time, not instantaneously. Nonetheless, he did dedicate himself to forgiveness and reconciliation, and served as the symbol of those things to his country.

The themes that underlie the story about Mandela and his efforts to reconcile with his captors are also present in Paul's letter to Philemon. The letter to Philemon is partially about reconciliation and forgiveness—reconciliation and forgiveness between a person who holds power over another, and that subjugated person. In particular, it concerns a master and his slave, and the complications that occur when someone is asked to forgive someone else's sin.

Before I go too far, I cannot look at the letter to Philemon without remembering that, not too long ago, this book was used by people to justify slavery in America. We have already discussed a few of the ways the Bible was used to justify slavery, but God's word is not a tool to subjugate people. People who used passages to justify slavery did not believe all people are worthy of love and compassion.

Ironically, Mandela admits that, early in his prison term, he did not see his tormentors as being equally created in God's eyes, either. Mandela said he was not able to forgive those inflicting pain on him until he began to see them as human, just as he was. He could only begin to forgive after he saw them as equal to him in God's eyes. That's partially what Paul was trying to communicate when he wrote his letter to Philemon: that, through God's eyes, everyone is equal and worthy of the same amount of love and compassion, regardless of their state in life.

To better understand what is going on in the letter to Philemon, we need to understand who Paul is writing to and why he's writing. Paul wrote this brief letter to Philemon, a well-to-do believer and friend who led a house church in a certain city. He was assisted by his wife and child, and Philemon had a positive reputation in the community because he was known for giving of his resources to the body of believers that regularly met in his home.

Philemon was also well-off enough to afford slaves, including one named Onesimus who had somehow rebelled against Philemon. We don't know exactly what Onesimus did, but we gather he may have run away, stole something and fled to a different city, or was sent away to perform a task, but didn't do it and never came home. Whatever the circumstance, it was public knowledge. Imagine being Philemon and a slave decided to do what they wanted instead of obeying your orders. And, then, imagine how it would feel if those around you, those closest to you, knew your circumstances.

Understand, slavery was not necessarily the same in those times as we think of in our nation's history. It was common during Philemon's time. According to Daniel Wallace, "As much as two thirds of the Roman empire were slaves (before the first century it was as high as 90%)."[7] Even Christians owned slaves. We don't understand how or why, but that was the reality. A person could become a slave as a spoil of war, a debt paid, or voluntarily to work off a debt. Since it was common, there were laws governing how slaves were to be treated. There were also laws in God's word showing slaves held intrinsic value and were worthy of a certain level of dignity.

There were communal laws protecting slaves, and also laws for punishment. If a slave failed to fulfill his duties/debts, his master could punish him; if a slave ran away, they would become "wanted" until they were found, at which point they could be sentenced to death or any other type of punishment their master might conceive. The person who found them could take custody of them, and if that person didn't, they could be charged with a crime.

According to Paul, Onesimus had experienced some type of transformation. Any change by Onesimus did not obligate Philemon to allow him to come back. Philemon had the right to hold a grudge against Onesimus, to exert certain authority over him, and to execute judgment against him.

What Paul is asking Philemon to do is to set all his rights aside and see and interact with Onesimus in an unusual way. Paul is asking him to forgive Onesimus and see him as more than just property, to see him as a brother in Christ. Paul does this in a few unique ways. Paul uses language associated with a slave to describe *himself*. Paul calls himself a slave of Christ. He opens the letter by calling himself a prisoner for Christ. He also calls himself a bond-servant for Christ. He essentially is saying he's in the same circumstances as Onesimus and he's no better than Onesimus. He challenges Philemon to view him and Onesimus the same.

Paul does this without directly describing Onesimus as a slave. Instead, he refers to him as his child, as someone who brings immense value to Paul's life. Paul is saying Onesimus brings immense value to other people's lives beyond what's expected. Onesimus is more than just a possession. He's a person making a substantial contribution on a personal level. Fundamentally, Paul is trying to bring about reconciliation. For Onesimus, it's his freedom and livelihood. If Philemon refuses, Onesimus can be subject to severe punishment. For Philemon, it's his reputation and influence in a community trying to figure out how faith in Christ should be lived out.

Holly Hearon says, "What I find fascinating about the letter [to Philemon] is the messiness of the situation it describes. It looks a lot like life as I know it. Relationships are messy. And, so often, it all depends on point of view."[8] Dr. Eric Barreto echoes this sentiment when he says:

> In the end, I'm convinced that Paul here is calling for a radical reorientation of the community's understanding of Onesimus' identity. He is no longer merely a cog in the machine of the household, no longer worthy because of the utility he provides for his master. Onesimus is now a beloved brother. He is kin. And this transformation is a vivid embodiment of the gospel. He is a walking reminder of the power of the good news. For Paul, what happens in these Christian communities is a matter of life and death. His letters are not just doctrinal. He's not just concerned with ideas, with the right Christological or theological or eschatological perspective. Paul is a pastor, remember. He cares for these communities because these communities are seeds of the resurrection, sites where the resurrected life can already flourish, places of resistance to an empire that would place us in rank according to social status.[9]

How does this apply to us? It's as much about reconciliation and forgiveness as it is about learning to view others as God does—regardless of skin color, economic status, education, or any other thing we use to keep ourselves separated. We may not think about it this way, but we all have Mandelas in our lives. We all have a Philemon or Onesimus in our past. We all have people we have not treated well. We have people who have not treated us well. And this affects us all in multiple ways.

These relationships, or lack thereof, affect our ability to trust others and God. This may sometimes be hard to recognize or admit. The sooner and more clearly we can recognize and work through the implications, the sooner and more clearly we can hear God speaking and leading us to experience life more abundantly.

Amen.

NOTES

Introduction

[1]James H. Cone, "Theology's Great Sin: Silence in the Face of White Supremacy," in *Theology in Global Context: Essays in Honor of Robert Cummings Neville*, ed. Amos Yong and Peter G. Heltzel (New York: T & T Clark International, 2004), 339.

[2]See https://www.cnn.com/2017/08/16/politics/blacks-white-racism-united-states-polls/index.html .

[3]Initial account online at https://www.kansas.com/news/article1065499.html .

[4]Account of settled lawsuit at http://www.nydailynews.com/news/national/parents-settle-lawsuit-pittsburgh-zoo-mauling-article-1.1814515 .

[5]See https://www.nwahomepage.com/news/knwa/child-in-critical-condition-after-falling-into-little-rock-zoo-jaguar-exhibit/147378892 .

[6]See https://www.cnn.com/2015/04/12/us/cleveland-zoo-cheetah-fall/index.html .

[7]See https://en.wikipedia.org/wiki/Killing_of_Harambe .

[8]Mark Ramsey, "'Did You See Their Faces?'" *Journal for Preachers* 39, no. 2 (2016): 29.

[9]See https://www.stltoday.com/pediatrician-s-baby-died-in-hot-car-in-st-louis/article_e3649c40-79e7-552a-960a-78f3d3f89f58.html .

[10]Gayraud S. Wilmore, "Black Messiah: Revising the Color Symbolism of Western Christology," *The Journal of the Interdenominational Theological Center* 2, no. 1 (September 1974): 9.

[11]David M. Katzman, *Before the Ghetto: Black Detroit in the Nineteenth Century* (Urbana, Ill.: University of Illinois Press, 1973), 208.

[12]David Sellery, "Holier Than Thou," *This Week's Focus*, http://us6.campaign-archive2.com/?u=dbffd2070718c7bb6a1b9b7e0&id=e7081ece52&e=9d753c1a09, accessed 6/12/16.

[13]John Martens, "Gospel: Welcome Sinners," *American: The Jesuit Review*, https://www.americamagazine.org/content/the-word/welcome-sinners, accessed 3/12/17.

[14]Clarence L. Cave, "Theological Significance of Racial and Cultural Pluralism," *Church & Society* 62, no. 5 (May 1972): 53.

[15]Paul Bellan-Boyer, "No Divisions?" *City Called Heaven* blog, http://citycalledheaven.blogspot.com/2011/01/no-divisions.html, accessed 1/23/11.

[16]Mary Hinkle Shore, "Commentary on 1 Corinthians 1:10–18," *Working Preacher*, https://www.workingpreacher.org/preaching.aspx?commentary_id=1998, accessed 1/26/14.

[17]Dwight Peterson, "Commentary on 1 Corinthians 1:10–18," *Working Preacher*, https://www.workingpreacher.org/preaching.aspx?commentary_id=26, accessed 1/26/14.

[18]Carol B. Franklin and Robert W. Tiller, "Racial Justice," *American Baptist Quarterly* 5, no. 1 (March 1986): 71.

Chapter 1: Roots of Our Racial Division

[1]W.E.B. Du Bois *The Souls of Black Folk,* ed. Brent Hayes Edwards. Oxford World's Classics (Oxford, England: Oxford University Press, 2007), 208.

[2]Reggie L. Williams, "Seeing Whiteness: Exercises in Understanding Race," *The Christian Century* 133, no. 15 (July 20, 2016): 25.

[3]Kenan Malik, *The Meaning of Race: Race, History, and Culture in Western Society* (New York: New York University Press, 1196), 126.

[4]Denton Lotz, *Baptists Against Racism* (Falls Church, Va.: Baptist World Alliance, 1999), 27.

[5]"NCCC Policy Statement on Racial Justice," *American Baptist Quarterly* 5, no. 1 (March 1986): 55.

[6]Ibid.

[7]Ibid.

[8]Robert Chambers, *Vestiges of the Natural History of Creation,* 2nd ed. (London: J. Churchill, 1844), 307.

[9]Charles Darwin, *The Voyage of the Beagle* (Auckland, New Zealand: Floating Press, 1839), 103.

[10]Charles Darwin, *The Descent of Man, and Selection in Relation to Sex* (London: Charles Murray, 1871), 105.

[11]George William Hunter, *A Civic Biology: Presented in Problems* (New York: American Book Company, 1914), 196.

[12]Robert Wilson Shufeldt, *The Negro: A Menace to American Civilization* (Boston: R.G. Badger, 1907), 43.

[13]Thomas Henry Huxley, *Collected Essays Volume III: Science and Education* (Cambridge, Eng.: Cambridge University Press. 2011), 66–67.

[14]Richard J. Herrnstein and Charles Murray, *The Bell Curve: Intelligence and Class Structure in American Life* (New York: Simon and Schuster, 1996), 91.

[15]Ibid.

[16]Richard J. Herrnstein and Charles Murray, as quoted in Jacoby, Russell, and Naomi Glauberman, *The Bell Curve Debate: History, Documents, Opinions* (New York: Times Books, 1998), 54.

[17]Joe Sims, "Flattening the Bell Curve," *People's Weekly World,* 1995, http://www.hartford-hwp.com/archives/45/023.html, accessed 3/20/2012.

[18]John Brown, quoted in Yuval Taylor, *I Was Born a Slave: An Anthology of Classic Slave Narratives,* Volume Two, 1849–1866 (Chicago: Lawrence Hill Books, 1999), 339.

[19]See https://www.history.com/news/the-infamous-40-year-tuskegee-study .

[20]Ira Glasser, "Racism Is Alive and Well and Living in Disguise," *Christianity and Crisis* 41, no. 5 (March 30, 1981): 74.

[21]Christopher Carter, "The Imago Dei as the Mind of Jesus Christ," *Zygon* 49, no. 3 (September 2014): 759.

[22]See https://www.britannica.com/topic/black-code

[23]Quoted in Frederic Jesup Stimson, *The Law of the Federal and State Constitutions of the United States: With an Historical Study of Their Principles, a Chronological Table of English Social Legislation, and a Comparative Digest of the Constitutions of the Forty-Six States* (Clark, N.J.: Lawbook Exchange, 2004), 118.

[24]Alexander C. Lichtenstein, *Twice the Work of Free Labor: The Political Economy of Convict Labor in the New South* New York: Verso, 1996), 3.

[25]Catherine Fisher Collins, *Black Girls and Adolescents: Facing the Challenges.* (Santa Barbara, Calif.: Praeger, 2015), 371.

[26]Judge Leon Bazile, as quoted in Werner Sollors, *Interracialism: Black-White Intermarriage in American History, Literature, and Law* (New York: Oxford University Press, 2000), 7.

[27]See http://www.presidency.ucsb.edu/ws/?pid=3188.

[28]See https://en.wikipedia.org/wiki/Fair_Sentencing_Act .

²⁹Duchess Harris, *Black Feminist Politics from Kennedy to Clinton* (New York: Palgrave Macmillan, 2011), 123.

³⁰James William Kilgore, *Understanding Mass Incarceration: A People's Guide to the Key Civil Rights Struggle of Our Time* (New York: The New Press, 2015), 33.

³¹Ibid., 35.

³²Alexia Cooper and Erica L. Smith, "Homicide Trends in the United States, 1980-2008," U.S. Department of Justice report, 2011, 13.

³³Robert M. Entman and Andrew Rojecki, *The Black Image in the White Mind: Media and Race in America* (Chicago: University of Chicago Press, 2001).

³⁴Kilgore, *Understanding Mass Incarceration*, 34.

³⁵Michael O. Emerson and Christian Smith, *Divided by Faith: Evangelical Religion and the Problem of Race in America* (New York: Oxford University Press, 2001), 22.

³⁶Bishop Edmund Gibson, as quoted in George W. Forell, ed., *Christian Social Teachings: A Reader in Christian Social Ethics from the Bible to the Present,* rev. and updated by James M. Childs (Minneapolis: Fortress Press, 2013), 361.

³⁷Emerson and Smith, *Divided by Faith,* 24.

Chapter 2: The Normality of Whiteness

¹Joseph R. Barndt, *Understanding and Dismantling Racism: The Twenty-First Century Challenge to White America* (Minneapolis: Fortress Press, 2007), 79.

²Jennifer Harvey, Karin A. Case, and Robin H. Gorsline, *Disrupting White Supremacy from Within: White People on What We Need to Do* (Cleveland: Pilgrim Press, 2004), 22.

³Reggie L. Williams, "Seeing Whiteness: Exercises in Understanding Race," *The Christian Century* 133, no. 15 (July 20, 2016): 25

⁴Cat Ngac Jonathan Tran, "The New Black Theology: Retrieving Ancient Sources to Challenge Racism," *The Christian Century* 129, no. 3 (February 8, 2012): 26.

⁵Harvey, Case, and Gorsline, *Disrupting White Supremacy from Within*, 4.

⁶James H. Cone, "Theology's Great Sin: Silence in the Face of White Supremacy," in *Theology in Global Context: Essays in Honor of Robert Cummings Neville,* ed. Amos Yong and Peter G. Heltzel (New York: T & T Clark, 2004), 346.

⁷Barbara J. Flagg, "'Was Blind but Now I See': White Race Consciousness and the Requirement of Discriminatory Intent," in *Critical White Studies: Looking Behind the Mirror,* ed. Richard Delgado and Jean Stefancic (Philadelphia: Temple University Press, 1997), 629.

⁸Ian Haney López, *White by Law: The Legal Construction of Race,* 10th anniv. ed. (New York: New York University Press, 2006).

⁹Willie J. Jennings, "Overcoming Racial Faith: How Christianity Became Entangled with Racism," in *Divinity Magazine,* Duke Divinity School (2015): 5.

¹⁰Ibid.

¹¹Ibid.

¹²Ibid., 7–8.

¹³http://www.dictionary.com/browse/manifest-destiny?s=t

¹⁴Jennings, "Overcoming."

¹⁵Anthony B. Pinn, "Jesus and Justice: An Outline of Liberation Theology within Black Churches," *Cross Currents* 57, no. 2 (2007): 218–19.

¹⁶Cone, "Theology's Great Sin,"340–41.

¹⁷Ibid., 341.

¹⁸Christopher Carter, "The Imago Dei as the Mind of Jesus Christ," *Zygon* 49, no. 3 (September 2014): 759.

¹⁹Willis N. Huggins and John G. Jackson, *An Introduction to African Civilizations, with Main Currents in Ethiopian History,* reprint (New York: Negro Universities Press, 1969), 55.

[20]Gayraud S. Wilmore, "Black Messiah: Revising the Color Symbolism of Western Christology," *The Journal of The Interdenominational Theological Center* 2, no. 1 (September 1974): 9.

[21]Ibid.

[22]Frank M. Snowden Jr., *Blacks in Antiquity: Ethiopians in the Greco-Roman Experience* (Cambridge, Mass., Belknap Press of Harvard University Press, 1970), 179.

[23]Wilmore, "Black Messiah," 10.

[24]Tran, "The New Black Theology," 24.

[25]Ibid.

[26]Eulalio R. Oaltazar, *The Dark Center: A Process Theology of Blackness* (New York: Paulist Press, 1973), 46.

[27]Dennis Hoekstra, "Ideology and Race Relations," *Reformed Journal* 14, no. 10 (December 1964): 17.

[28]Malina, Bruce J. *The New Testament World: Insights from Cultural Anthropology* (Louisville: Westminster John Knox Press, 2001), 62–63.

[29]Ibid.

[30]David M. May, "Mark 3:20–35 from the Perspective of Shame/Honor," *Biblical Theology Bulletin*, 17, no. 3 (1987): 80.

[31]Quoted in William R. Jones, *Is God a White Racist? A Preamble to Black Theology* (Garden City, N.Y.: Anchor Press, 1973), 5.

[32]James Baldwin, *Price of the Ticket: Collected Nonfiction, 1948–1985* New York: St. Martin's/Marek, 1985), 88.

[33]Jennings, "Overcoming Racial Faith," 9.

[34]Edward M. Huenemann, "Reflections of a White Presbyterian Theologian on the Black Messiah," *Church & Society* 72, no. 4 (March 1982): 6.

[35]Peter Goodwin Heltzel, *Jesus and Justice: Evangelicals, Race, and American Politics* (New Haven: Yale University Press, 2009), 204.

[36]See https://religionnews.com/2018/07/02/why-white-evangelicals-voted-for-trump-fear-power-and-nostalgia/ .

[37]Kristin Du Mez, "Donald Trump and Militant Evangelical Masculinity," *Religion and Politics*, http://religionandpolitics.org/2017/01/17/donald-trump-and-militant-evangelical-masculinity/, accessed 2/1/17.

[38]Ta-Nehisi Coates, "The First White President," *The Atlantic*, (October 2017), https://www.theatlantic.com/magazine/archive/2017/10/the-first-white-president-ta-nehisi-coates/537909/, accessed 9/18/17.

[39]Cone, "Theology's Great Sin," 344.

[40]Ibid., 345.

[41]Ibid., 347.

[42]Ibid., 346.

[43]Ibid., 344.

[44]Michael O. Emerson and Christian Smith, *Divided by Faith: Evangelical Religion and the Problem of Race in America* (New York: Oxford University Press, 2001), 74.

[45]Michael Emerson, "Faith That Separates: Evangelicals and Black-White Race Relations," in *A Public Faith: Evangelicals and Civic Engagement*, ed. Michael Cromartie (Lanham, Md.: Rowman & Littlefield, 2003), quoted in Geoffrey N. Schoonmaker, *Preaching about Race: A Homiletic for Racial Reconciliation* (dissertation, Vanderbilt University, 2012), 26.

[46]Schoonmaker, *Preaching about Race*, 26.

[47]Ibid.

[48]Ibid, 13.

[49]Ibid., 9.

[50]Mark A. Noll, *The Scandal of the Evangelical Mind* (Grand Rapids, Mich.: William B. Eerdmans, 1994), 12.

[51]Schoonmaker, *Preaching about Race*, 26.

⁵²Noll, *Scandal of the Evangelical Mind*, 32.

⁵³Schoonmaker, *Preaching about Race*, 18–21.

⁵⁴Eric Tranby and Douglas Hartmann, "Critical Whiteness Theories and the Evangelical 'Race Problem': Extending Emerson and Smith's *Divided by Faith*," *Journal for the Scientific Study of Religion* 47, no. 3 (2008): 354.

⁵⁵Cromartie, *A Public Faith*, 197.

⁵⁶John C. Green, Robert P. Jones, Daniel Cox, "Faithful, Engaged, and Divergent: A Comparative Portrait of Conservative and Progressive Religious Activists in the 2008 Election and Beyond," (University of Akron and Public Religion Research, 2009), available online at https://www.uakron.edu/bliss/research/archives/2008/ReligiousActivistReport-Final.pdf .

⁵⁷Emerson and Smith, *Divided by Faith*, 117.

⁵⁸Ira Glasser, "Racism Is Alive and Well and Living in Disguise," *Christianity and Crisis* 41, no. 5 (March 30, 1981): 68.

⁵⁹Cone, "Theology's Great Sin," 347.

⁶⁰Ibid., 349.

⁶¹Glasser, "Racism Is Alive and Well," 68.

⁶²Ibid.

⁶³Cone, "Theology's Great Sin," 340–41.

⁶⁴Clarence L. Cave, "Theological Significance of Racial and Cultural Pluralism," *Church & Society* 62, no. 5 (May 1972): 54.

Chapter 3: Aftereffects

¹Clarence L. Cave, "Theological Significance of Racial and Cultural Pluralism," *Church & Society* 62, no. 5 (May 1972): 53.

²All quotes that follow from Jennifer Richeson and statistical information come from William Wan and Sarah Kaplan, "Why Are People Still Racist?: What Science Says about America's Race Problem," *Washington Post*, https://www.washingtonpost.com/news/speaking-of-science/wp/2017/08/14/why-are-people-still-racist-what-science-says-about-americas-race-problem/?utm_term=.84611ea89d2c, accessed August 14, 2017.

³Alvin Chang, "White America Is Quietly Self-Segregating," *Vox*, https://www.vox.com/2017/1/18/14296126/white-segregated-suburb-neighborhood-cartoon, accessed 2/12/17

⁴Ibid.

⁵Ibid.

⁶Ibid.

⁷Ibid.

⁸Ta-Nehisi Coates, "The First White President," *The Atlantic* (October 2017), https://www.theatlantic.com/magazine/archive/2017/10/the-first-white-president-ta-nehisi-coates/537909/, accessed 9/18/17.

⁹Ibid.

¹⁰A.L. Higginbotham, *In the Matter of Color: Race and the American Legal Process: The Colonial Period* (New York: Oxford University Press, 1980), 276.

¹¹Terrence Cunningham, as quoted in Julia Craven, "National Police Group Apologizes for Past Racial Injustices, but Not Current Ones," *Huffington Post*, http://www.huffingtonpost.com/entry/iacp-police-racism-apology_us_58054347e4b0b994d4c0f326, accessed 10/17/16.

¹²Ibid.

¹³Brian Peterson, "Commentary on 1 Corinthians 12:1–31a," *Working Preacher*, https://www.workingpreacher.org/preaching.aspx?commentary_id=2733, accessed 1/24/16.

¹⁴Holly Hearon, "Commentary on 2 Corinthians 5:16–21," *Working Preacher*, https://www.workingpreacher.org/preaching.aspx?commentary_id=535, accessed 3/14/10.

Chapter 4: Finding Common Ground

[1]Christopher Carter, "The Imago Dei as the Mind of Jesus Christ," *Zygon* 49, no. 3 (September 2014): 759.

[2]Richard Delgado and Jean Stefancic, *Critical Race Theory: An Introduction* (New York: New York University Press, 2001), 7.

[3]Jeffrey N. Schoonmaker, *Preaching about Race: A Homiletic for Racial Reconciliation* (dissertation, Vanderbilt University, 2012), 30.

[4]Michael O. Emerson and Christian Smith, *Divided by Faith: Evangelical Religion and the Problem of Race in America* (New York: Oxford University Press, 2001), 89.

[5]Barbara J. Flagg, "'Was Blind But Now I See': White Race Consciousness and the Requirement of Discriminatory Intent," In *Critical White Studies: Looking Behind the Mirror,* ed. Richard Delgado and Jean Stefancic (Philadelphia: Temple University Press, 1997), 629.

[6]Schoonmaker, *Preaching about Race,* 13.

[7]Walter Kim, "Theology of Race Interview," National Association of Evangelicals website, https://www.nae.net/kimpodcast/, accessed 7/12/16.

[8]Schoonmaker, *Preaching about Race,* 28.

[9]Psychology professor Eric Knowles, quoted in William Wan and Sarah Kaplan, "Why Are People Still Racist?: What Science says about America's Race Problem," *Washington Post,* https://www.washingtonpost.com/news/speaking-of-science/wp/2017/08/14/why-are-people-still-racist-what-science-says-about-americas-race-problem/?utm_term=.84611ea89d2c, accessed August 14, 2017

[10]Michael Emerson, William Mirola, and Susanne C. Monahan, *Religion Matters: What Sociology Teaches Us About Religion In Our World* (New York: Routledge, 2016), 163.

[11]Martin Luther King Jr., *Dream: The Words and Inspiration of Martin Luther King, Jr.,* (Boulder, Colo.: Blue Mountain Press, 2007), 46.

[12]Emerson, Mirola, and Monahan, *Religion Matters,* 163.

[13]Ryon J. Cobb, Samuel L. Perry, and Kevin D. Dougherty, "United by Faith?: Race/Ethnicity, Congregational Diversity, and Explanations of Racial Inequality," *Sociology Of Religion* 76, no. 2 (2015): 180.

[14]Michael O. Emerson, "A New Day for Multiracial Congregations," *Reflections,* Yale University, 2013, http://reflections.yale.edu/article/future-race/new-day-multiracial-congregations, accessed 2/12/2014.

[15]Ibid.

[16]Ibid.

[17]Ibid.

[18]Ibid.

[19]Cobb, Perry, and Dougherty, "United by Faith?" 179–80.

[20]Ibid., 180.

[21]Ibid., 193.

[22]Ibid. 195–96.

[23]James H. Cone, "Theology's Great Sin: Silence in the Face of White Supremacy," in *Theology in Global Context: Essays in Honor of Robert Cummings Neville,* ed. Amos Yong and Peter G. Heltzel (New York: T & T Clark International, 2004,) 350.

[24]Schoonmaker, *Preaching about Race,* 32, 38.

[25]C. Anthony Hunt, "I've Seen the Promised Land: The Legacy of Martin Luther King, Jr., and Prophetic Preaching," *Hope for the City* blog, http://newurbanministry.blogspot.com/2016/04/ive-seen-promised-land-legacy-of-martin.html, accessed 4/24/16.

[26]Pamela Baker Powell, "The Lord in Black Skin," *Christianity Today* 44, no. 11 (October 2, 2000): 54.

[27]Quoted in Emerson, "A New Day for Multiracial Congregations."

[28]Ibid.

[29]Cone, "Theology's Great Sin," 350.

[30]Ibid.

[31]Rabbi Joachim Prinz, quoted in James Cone, "Theology's Great Sin: Silence in the Face of White Supremacy," in *The Cambridge Companion to Black Theology*, ed. Dwight Hopkins and Edward P. Antonio (New York: Cambridge University Press, 2012), 153.

[32]Cone, "Theology's Great Sin," in *Theology in Global Context*, 345.

[33]Ibid., 351.

[34]Joel Schreurs, "Beyond the Lectionary Text: Jonah 1—4," Center for Excellence in Preaching website, http://cep.calvinseminary.edu/non-rcl-starters/jonah-1-4/, accessed 4/12/17.

[35]Ibid.

[36]Beth L. Tanner, "Commentary on Jonah 3:1–5, 10," *Working Preacher*, https://www.workingpreacher.org/preaching.aspx?commentary_id=229, accessed 1/27/09.

[37]Ibid.

[38]William Carter, "When God Repented," Day 1 website, http://day1.org/698-when_god_repented, accessed 7/12/02.

[39]Frances Flannery, "The Challenge of Jonah: Countering Radicalization Through Radical Inclusion," *Huffington Post*, http://www.huffingtonpost.com/frances-flannery/the-challenge-of-jonah-countering-radicalization-through-radical-inclusion_b_8807608.html, accessed 11/17/16.

[40]John Holbert, "Prophet Gone Bad: Reflections on Jonah 3:1–5," *Patheos*, http://www.patheos.com/progressive-christian/prophet-gone-bad-john-c-holbert-01-19-2015.aspx?p=2, accessed 2/23/16.

[41]Ibid.

Conclusion

[1]Christopher Carter, "The Imago Dei as the Mind of Jesus Christ," *Zygon* 49, no. 3 (September 2014): 759–60.

[2]David Anderson, "Public Life and Good Works (Titus 3:1–2)," Bible.org website, https://bible.org/seriespage/7-public-life-and-good-works-titus-31-2, accessed 6/15/17.

[3]Francis of Assisi, as quoted in Scott Gallagher, *Words of Wisdom: A Thinker's Palette* (CreateSpace, 2011), 60.

[4]Gregory Ledbetter, "Galatians 2:15–21: Homiletical Perspective," in *Feasting on the Word, Year C, Volume 3*, ed. David L. Bartlett, and Barbara Brown (Louisville: Westminster John Knox Press, 2010), 137.

[5]Alicia Vargas, "Commentary on Galatians 2:15–21," *Working Preacher*, https://www.workingpreacher.org/preaching.aspx?commentary_id=2872, accessed 6/12/16.

[6]Alan Brehm, "Helping Ourselves?" The Waking Dreamer blog, http://thewakingdreamer.blogspot.com/2010/06/helping-ourselves-gal-215-21-lk-726-50.html, accessed 12/3/13.

[7]See https://bible.org/article/some-initial-reflections-slavery-new-testament.

[8]Holly Hearon, "Commentary on Philemon 1:1–21," *Working Preacher*, https://www.workingpreacher.org/preaching.aspx?commentary_id=669, accessed 7/12/13.

[9]Eric Barreto, "Commentary on Philemon 1:1–21," *Working Preacher*, https://www.workingpreacher.org/preaching.aspx?commentary_id=2975

SELECTED RESOURCES

Anderson, David. "Public Life and Good Works (Titus 3:1–2)." Bible.org website. https://bible.org/seriespage/7-public-life-and-good-works-titus-31-2. Accessed 6/15/17.

Baldwin, James. *Price of the Ticket: Collected Nonfiction, 1948–1985*. New York: St. Martin's/Marek, 1985.

Barndt, Joseph R. *Understanding and Dismantling Racism: The Twenty-First Century Challenge to White America*. Minneapolis: Fortress Press, 2007.

Barreto, Eric. "Commentary on Philemon 1:1–21." *Working Preacher*. https://www.workingpreacher.org/preaching aspx? commentary_id=2975. Accessed 9/9/16.

Bellan-Boyer, Paul. "No Divisions?" City Called Heaven blog. http://citycalledheaven.blogspot.com/2011/01/no-divisions.html. Accessed 1/23/11.

Brehm, Alan. "Helping Ourselves?" The Waking Dreamer blog. http://thewakingdreamer.blogspot.com/2010/06/helping-ourselves-gal-215-21-lk-726-50.html. Accessed 12/3/13.

Carter, Christopher. "The Imago Dei as the Mind of Jesus Christ." *Zygon* 49, no. 3, 2014.

Carter, Terrell. *Walking the Blue Line: A Police Officer Turned Community Activist Provides Solutions to the Racial Divide*. Bettie Youngs Books, 2015.

Carter, William. "When God Repented." Day 1 website. http://day1.org/698-when_god_repented. Accessed 7/12/02.

Cave, Clarence L. "Theological Significance of Racial and Cultural Pluralism." *Church & Society* 62, no. 5, May 1972.

Chambers, Robert. *Vestiges of the Natural History of Creation*. 2nd ed. London: J. Churchill, 1844.

Chang, Alvin. "White America Is Quietly Self-Segregating." *Vox*. https://www.vox.com/2017/1/18/14296126/white-segregated-suburb-neighborhood-cartoon, Accessed 2/12/17.

Coates, Ta-Nehisi. "The First White President." *The Atlantic,* October 2017. https://www.theatlantic.com/magazine/archive/2017/10/the-first-white-president-ta-nehisi-coates/537909/. Accessed 9/18/17.

Cobb, Ryon J., Samuel L. Perry, and Kevin D. Dougherty. "United by Faith?: Race/Ethnicity, Congregational Diversity, and Explanations of Racial Inequality." *Sociology of Religion* 76, no. 2, 2015.

Collins, Catherine Fisher. *Black Girls and Adolescents: Facing the Challenges.* Santa Barbara, Calif.: Praeger, 2015.

Cone, James H. "Theology's Great Sin: Silence in the Face of White Supremacy." In *Theology in Global Context: Essays in Honor of Robert Cummings Neville.* Edited by Amos Yong and Peter G. Heltzel. New York: T & T Clark, 2004.

———— "Theology's Great Sin." In *The Cambridge Companion to Black Theology.* Edited by Dwight Hopkins and Edward P. Antonio. New York: Cambridge University Press, 2012.

Craven, Julia. "National Police Group Apologizes for Past Racial Injustices, but Not Current Ones." *Huffington Post.* http://www.huffingtonpost.com/entry/iacp-police-racism-apology_us_58054347e4b0b994d4c0f326. Accessed 10/17/16.

Cromartie, Michael. *A Public Faith: Evangelicals and Civic Engagement.* Lanham, Md.: Rowman & Littlefield, 2003.

Darwin, Charles. *The Descent of Man and Selection in Relation to Sex.* London: Charles Murray, 1871.

———— *The Voyage of the Beagle.* Auckland, New Zealand: Floating Press, 1839.

Dirck, Brian R. *The Executive Branch of Federal Government: People, Process, and Politics.* Santa Barbara, Calif.: ABC-CLIO, 2007.

Du Bois, W.E.B., and Brent Hayes Edwards. *The Souls of Black Folk.* Oxford World's Classics. Oxford, England: Oxford University Press, 2007.

Du Mez, Kristin. "Donald Trump and Militant Evangelical Masculinity." *Religion and Politics.* http://religionand

politics.org/2017/01/17/donald-trump-and-militant-evangelical-masculinity/. Accessed 2/1/17.

Editors of Encyclopedia Britannica. "Black Code." *Encyclopedia Britannica*. https://www.britannica.com/topic/black-code. Accessed August 3, 2017.

Emerson, Michael O. "A New Day for Multiracial Congregations." *Reflections*. Yale University, 2013. http://reflections.yale.edu/article/future-race/new-day-multiracial-congregations. Accessed 2/12/2014.

————, and Christian Smith. *Divided by Faith: Evangelical Religion and the Problem of Race in America*. New York: Oxford University Press, 2001.

————, William Mirola, and Susanne C. Monahan. *Religion Matters: What Sociology Teaches Us About Religion in Our World*. London: Routledge, 2016.

Flagg, Barbara J. "'Was Blind but Now I See': White Race Consciousness and the Requirement of Discriminatory Intent." In *Critical White Studies: Looking Behind the Mirror*. Edited by Richard Delgado and Jean Stefancic. Philadelphia: Temple University Press, 1997.

Flannery, Frances. "The Challenge of Jonah: Countering Radicalization Through Radical Inclusion." *Huffington Post*. http://www.huffingtonpost.com/frances-flannery/the-challenge-of-jonah-countering-radicalization-through-radical-inclusion_b_8807608.html. Accessed 11/17/16.

Forell, George W. *Christian Social Teachings: A Reader in Christian Social Ethics from the Bible to the Present*. Minneapolis: Fortress Press, 2012.

Franklin, Carol B., and Robert W. Tiller. "Racial Justice." *American Baptist Quarterly* 5, no. 1, March 1986.

Gallagher, Scott. *Words of Wisdom: A Thinker's Palette*. Self-published, CreateSpace, 2011.

Glasser, Ira. "Racism Is Alive and Well and Living in Disguise." *Christianity and Crisis* 41, no. 5, 1981.

Haney-López, Ian F. *White by Law: The Legal Construction of Race*. New York: New York University Press, 2006.

Harris, Duchess. *Black Feminist Politics from Kennedy to Clinton*. New York: Palgrave Macmillan, 2011.

Harvey, Jennifer, Karin A. Case, and Robin H. Gorsline. *Disrupting White Supremacy from Within: White People on What We Need to Do.* Cleveland: Pilgrim Press, 2008.

Hearon, Holly. "Commentary on 2 Corinthians 5:16–21." *Working Preacher.* https://www.workingpreacher. org/preaching.aspx?commentary_id=535.   Accessed 3/14/10.

———. "Commentary on Philemon 1:1–21." *Working Preacher.*   https://www.workingpreacher.org/ preaching.aspx?commentary_id=669.   Accessed 7/12/13.

Heltzel, Peter. *Jesus and Justice: Evangelicals, Race, and American Politics.* New Haven: Yale University Press, 2009.

Herrnstein, Richard J., and Charles Murray. *Bell Curve: Intelligence and Class Structure in American Life.* New York: Simon and Schuster, 1996.

Higginbotham, A.L. *In the Matter of Color: Race and the American Legal Process. The Colonial Period.* New York: Oxford University Press, 1980.

Hoekstra, Dennis. "Ideology and Race Relations." *Reformed Journal* 14, no. 10, 1964.

Holbert, John. "Prophet Gone Bad: Reflections on Jonah 3:1–5." *Patheos.* http://www.patheos.com/progressive-christian/prophet-gone-bad-john-c-holbert-01-19-2015. aspx?p=2. Accessed 2/23/16.

Huenemann, Edward M. "Reflections of a White Presbyterian Theologian on the Black Messiah." *Church & Society* 72, no. 4, 1982.

Huggins, Willis N., and John G. Jackson. *An Introduction to African Civilizations.* New York: Negro Universities Press, 1969.

Hunt, C. Anthony. "I've Seen the Promised Land: The Legacy of Martin Luther King, Jr., and Prophetic Preaching." *Hope for the City* blog. http://newurbanministry. blogspot.com/2016/04/ive-seen-promised-land-legacy-of-martin.html. Accessed 4/24/16.

Hunter, George William. *A Civic Biology: Presented in Problems.* New York: American Book Company, 1914.

Huxley, Thomas Henry. *Collected Essays Volume III: Science and Education*. Edited by Leonard Huxley. Reprint edition. New York: Cambridge University Press, 2011.

Jacoby, Russell, and Naomi Glauberman. *The Bell Curve Debate: History, Documents, Opinions*. New York: Times Books, 1998.

Jennings, Willie J. "Overcoming Racial Faith: How Christianity Became Entangled with Racism." *Divinity Magazine*. Duke Divinity School, 2015.

Jones, William R. *Is God a White Racist? A Preamble to Black Theology*. Garden City, N.Y.: Anchor Press, 1973.

Katzman, David M. *Before the Ghetto: Black Detroit in the Nineteenth Century*. Urbana: University of Illinois Press, 1973.

Kilgore, James William. *Understanding Mass Incarceration: A People's Guide to the Key Civil Rights Struggle of Our Time*. New York: The New Press, 2015.

Kim, Walter. "Theology of Race Interview," National Association of Evangelicals website. https://www.nae.net/kimpodcast/. Accessed 7/12/16.

King, Martin Luther, Jr. *Dream: The Words and Inspiration of Martin Luther King, Jr.* Boulder, Colo.: Blue Mountain Press, 2007.

Ledbetter, Gregory, David L. Bartlett, and Barbara Brown. *Feasting on the Word, Year C, Volume 3*. Louisville: Westminster John Knox Press, 2010.

Lichtenstein, Alexander C. *Twice the Work of Free Labor: The Political Economy of Convict Labor in the New South*. New York: Verso, 1996.

Lotz, Denton. *Baptists Against Racism*. Falls Church, Va.: Baptist World Alliance, 1999.

Malik, Kenan. *The Meaning of Race: Race, History, and Culture in Western Society*. New York: New York University Press, 1996.

Malina, Bruce J. *The New Testament World*. Louisville: Westminster John Knox Press, 2001.

Martens, John. "Gospel: Welcome Sinners," *American: The Jesuit Review*. https://www.americamagazine.org/content/the-word/welcome-sinners. Accessed 3/12/17.

May, David M. "Mark 3:20–35 from the Perspective of Shame/Honor." *Biblical Theology Bulletin* 17, no. 3, 1987.

"NCCC Policy Statement on Racial Justice." *American Baptist Quarterly* 5, no. 1, 1986.

Nixon, Richard. "Annual Budget Message to the Congress, Fiscal Year 1972." The American Presidency Project. http://www.presidency.ucsb.edu/ws/?pid=3188. Accessed 8/6/17.

Noll, Mark A. *The Scandal of the Evangelical Mind.* Grand Rapids, Mich.: William B. Eerdmans Publishing Company, 1994.

Oaltazar, Eulalio R. *The Dark Center: A Process Theology of Blackness.* New York: Paulist Press, 1973.

Peterson, Brian. "Commentary on 1 Corinthians 12:1–31a." *Working Preacher.* https://www.workingpreacher.org/preaching.aspx?commentary_id=2733. Accessed 1/24/16.

Peterson, Dwight. "Commentary on 1 Corinthians 1:10–18." *Working Preacher.* https://www.workingpreacher.org/preaching.aspx?commentary_id=26. Accessed 1/26/14.

Pinn, Anthony B. "Jesus and Justice: an Outline of Liberation Theology within Black Churches." *Cross Currents* 57, no. 2, 2007.

Powell, Pamela Baker. "The Lord in Black Skin." *Christianity Today* 44, no. 11, 2000.

Ramsey, Mark. "'Did You See Their Faces?'" *Journal for Preachers* 39, no. 2, 2016.

Schoonmaker, Jeffrey N. (Dissertation) *Preaching about Race: A Homiletic for Racial Reconciliation.* Vanderbilt University, 2012.

Schreurs, Joel. "Beyond the Lectionary Text: Jonah 1—4." Center for Excellence in Preaching website. http://cep.calvinseminary.edu/non-rcl-starters/jonah-1-4/. Accessed 4/12/17.

Sellery, David. "Holier Than Thou." *This Week's Focus.* http://us6.campaign-archive2.com/?u=dbffd2070718c7bb6a1b9b7e0&id=e7081ece52&e=9d753c1a09. Accessed 6/12/16.

Shore, Mary Hinkle. "Commentary on 1 Corinthians 1:10–18." *Working Preacher*. https://www.workingpreacher.org/preaching.aspx?commentary_id=1998.   Accessed 1/26/14.

Shufeldt, Robert Wilson. *The Negro: A Menace to American Civilization*. Boston: R.G. Badger, 1907.

Sims, Joe. "Flattening the Bell Curve." *People's Weekly World*. 1995. http://www.hartford-hwp.com/archives/45/023.html. Accessed 3/20/2012.

Snowden, Frank M. Jr., *Blacks in Antiquity*. Cambridge, Mass.: Belknap Press of Harvard University Press, 1970.

Sollors, Werner. *Interracialism: Black-White Intermarriage in American History, Literature, and Law*. New York: Oxford University Press, 2000.

Stimson, Frederic Jesup. *The Law of the Federal and State Constitutions of the United States: With an Historical Study of Their Principles, a Chronological Table of English Social Legislation, and a Comparative Digest of the Constitutions of the Forty-Six States*. Clark, N.J.: Lawbook Exchange, 2004.

Struyk, Ryan. "Blacks and whites see racism in the United States very, very differently." CNN.com. https://www.cnn.com/2017/08/16/politics/blacks-white-racism-united-states-polls/index.html Accessed 8/18/2017.

Tanner, Beth L. "Commentary on Jonah 3:1–5, 10." *Working Preacher*. https://www.workingpreacher.org/preaching.aspx?commentary_id=229.   Accessed 1/27/09.

Taylor, Yuval. *I Was Born a Slave: An Anthology of Classic Slave Narratives, Volume Two, 1849–1866*. Chicago: Lawrence Hill Books, 1999.

Tran, Cat Ngac Jonathan. "The New Black Theology: Retrieving Ancient Sources to challenge Racism." *The Christian Century* 129, no. 3, 2012.

Tranby, Eric, and Douglas Hartmann. "Critical Whiteness Theories and the Evangelical 'Race Problem': Extending Emerson and Smith's *Divided by Faith*." *Journal for the Scientific Study of Religion* 47, no. 3, 2008.

Vargas, Alicia. "Commentary on Galatians 2:15–21." *Working Preacher.* https://www.workingpreacher. org/preaching.aspx?commentary_id=2872.   Accessed 6/12/16.

Wallace, Daniel B, "Some Initial Reflections on Slavery in the New Testament." Bible.org. https://bible.org/ article/some-initial-reflections-slavery-new-testament. Accessed 6/1/17.

Wan, William, and Sarah Kaplan, "Why Are People Still Racist?: What Science Says about America's Race Problem." *Washington Post.* https://www. washingtonpost.com/news/speaking-of-science/ wp/2017/08/14/why-are-people-still-racist-what-science-says-about-americas-race-problem/?utm_ term=.84611ea89d2c. Accessed August 14, 2017.

Williams, Reggie L. "Seeing Whiteness: Exercises in Understanding Race." *The Christian Century* 133, no. 15, 2016.

Wilmore, Gayraud S. "Black Messiah: Revising the Color Symbolism of Western Christology." *The Journal of The Interdenominational Theological Center* 2, no. 1, 1974.